THE AUTHOR

Recently retired as Horace Bushnell professor of Christian nurture at Yale Divinity School, Paul H. Vieth has used his "leisure" to serve as a visiting professor at such schools as Andover Newton Theological School and Union Theological Seminary of New York. He is a member of the Division of Christian Education of the National Council of Churches and of the World Council of Christian Education. He is also the superintendent of a local church school.

Dr. Vieth holds degrees from Central Wesleyan College, Yale Divinity School, and the Graduate School of Yale University. He lists "Christian education" as his vocation. He has served as general secretary of the Missouri Church Council; director of Christian education at the Church of the Redeemer, New Haven, Connecticut; director of research for the former International Council of Religious Education; and editor of the *International Journal of Religious Education*.

During 1947-48 he was Adviser on Religious Education for the Supreme Commander of Allied Powers in Japan. In 1954-55 he taught at the International Christian University in Tokyo, as a Fulbright scholar.

Some of his previous books are *The Church School, The Church and Christian Education, Teaching for Christian Living,* and *How to Teach in the Church School.*

WORSHIP IN CHRISTIAN EDUCATION

Paul H. Vieth

Worship in
Christian Education

UNITED CHURCH PRESS
PHILADELPHIA BOSTON

FOREWORD

Christian education and worship are insep-
arably related. Neither is complete or most effective without the other. To speak more exactly, Christian education
includes and comes to its highest expression in worship,
and worship leads into and is supported by Christian education.

Christian education in its practical aspects is so much
affected by the maturity of the persons with whom it deals,
so different in various age-groups, that it may be ques-
tioned whether any general book on worship can serve a
useful purpose. This book has been written in the conviction that such a general treatment is not only possible, but
that it meets a distinct need. This conviction is supported
by such considerations as:

Christian education today is extremely sensitive to its
setting within the whole church fellowship. What concerns
the church also concerns its Christian educators. The
church school can no longer carry on an independent life

but is conditioned by all that the church is and does. This includes its corporate worship.

The nature of worship does not vary with the age of worshipers, even though the forms and materials through which it is experienced do vary with different stages of maturity.

The worship life of the church is centered around the corporate worship of the congregation—not a congregation of the mature only, but of the whole family in the Christian fellowship. Christian education is not a venture apart from this but must be in vital relation to it. Worship in the church school is not an independent parallel activity but is intimately related to the church at worship through following the same general principles and through educating the pupils for participation therein.

The worship aspect of the curriculum should be planned in the perspective of the total worship life of the church. This requires that the committee on Christian education and the church school officers deal with the problem as a whole, not in piecemeal departmental fashion.

Leaders of worship in the church school, no matter what the age of their pupils, need to gain insight into and understanding of the general nature and meaning of worship as a sound basis for planning and leading in their own groups.

The first seven chapters of this book treat the subject as a whole, with incidental references to how these general considerations apply to church school groups of different ages. The remainder of the book is devoted to worship practice in the several departments of the church school with a view to making specific application of the general understanding and principles.

This book is addressed primarily to the lay men and women who are responsible for planning and conducting worship in the church school—members of the committee on Christian education, general officers, department and class leaders, and young people who plan and lead the worship activities in their church school and youth groups. Pastors should find those sections helpful which deal with the relation of the church school to the church service, and with family services.

It is hoped that *all* church school workers will profit from the reading of this book, in understanding the place of worship in the curriculum, in cooperating with the leaders of worship, and in guiding pupils to achieve reality and sincerity in their worship experience.

PAUL H. VIETH

CONTENTS

1 WORSHIP IN CHRISTIAN EDUCATION

The worship of God is the noblest achievement of man, and the focal point in the life and work of the Christian church. This was implied many years ago in *The Shorter Catechism.*

Question: What is the chief end of man?

Answer: Man's chief end is to glorify God and enjoy him forever.

Another way in which this answer might be worded is "To worship God and to live for him."

The worship life of the church comes to fullest expression in the Lord's Day liturgy, when the whole congregation gathers to celebrate the glory and grace of God, in thankfulness for what he is doing for man, and in renewal of commitment to his will. But worship is not limited to this one event in which the whole congregation participates. The church includes many groups in which worship is a part of the program, such as church school departments

11

and classes, youth groups, men's and women's groups—to name but a few.

Our first concern is that such groups may have a genuine experience of Christian worship. A further concern is that through such experience persons may learn the joy of worship and the ability to participate effectively in a worshiping congregation. Worship is included in such groups so that they may "glorify God and enjoy him forever," but it also has a lead-in purpose to facilitate participation in the worship life of the congregation. Worship has a proper place in the program of educational groups, but never as a substitute for worshiping with the whole congregation (except, perhaps, in the case of young children).

WORSHIP IN THE CURRICULUM

All church schools include worship as a part of the program. In some churches the whole church school meets together for worship, but this practice is increasingly rare. In most churches worship is conducted by department groups. Many teachers also include worship as an integral part of the class session, either in addition to a department service or without such a department assembly.

It is usually expected that teachers and pupils will also attend the general service of worship of the church. In many cases such attendance at "church" is planned as a part of the curriculum, in the form of a regular or occasional "family service," or by some other plan which assures that pupils will have some experience in the corporate worship of the church. More often church attendance is but a hopeful expectation, realized in widely varying degrees in different churches.

Why is worship so much a part of the curriculum of Christian education? Is it because this is the traditional way of doing things? Is it merely because it is felt that when people come together in the church there should be worship, even though it is but perfunctory and preliminary to the "main business" of their coming? Judging by the casual way in which worship is treated in many church schools and other groups, these questions are not too far afield. Training for leaders of worship is greatly behind the training of teachers. It is only in recent years that curriculum materials have offered helps for worship which are at all comparable to the helps for teaching.

Let us state the case more positively: *Christian worship is the most significant element in the curriculum of Christian education.* Without it, that which we do is not truly *Christian* education. In support of this contention, we offer the following considerations:

1. Christian faith, and hence Christian education, is focused on God and his relation to man. It affirms God as the Creator and Sustainer of the universe, and man as his dependent creature. It affirms that God reveals himself to man, and that man has been so created that he can respond to and have communion with God. This faith is attested to in prayers and hymns and other elements in the service of worship. Worship is the living expression of the faith which is taught, and also provides the basic orientation for Christian teaching.

2. Worship is the highest outcome of Christian education, and at the same time a means for giving it vitality and meaning. Man's relation to God and man's obligation under God are both brought into focus in worship. If God is not a living reality in worship, how can he be adequately served and taught?

3. Worship is at the heart of what the church is and

13

does. "The single unique function of the church is the worshiping of God. This is one activity no other group attempts."[1] Other things which the church does are necessary and important—teaching, fellowship, service, recreation, financing—but they are also done by other institutions. It is only the church which provides for people to gather at regular intervals for the worship of God.

What this means for Christian education should be clear. One of its major purposes is to prepare persons for, introduce them into, and help them find meaningful life in the church. Roger Shinn has suggested that one way of expressing the purpose of Christian education is: "To introduce persons into the life and mission of the community of Christian faith."[2] This cannot be accomplished without adequate attention to and participation in the worship life of the church.

4. Worship as an element in the curriculum is more than preparation for an experience of worship outside the curriculum. Christian education is not just preparation for living the Christian life, but actual experience in living as a Christian. To worship God is a basic human need, as real as the need for food and human companionship and other values that give life meaning. This is as true for the young child as for the mature man or woman. Hence the opportunity to worship is properly included as an integral part of Christian education.

5. There is need for education in worship. While the impulse to worship is deep-seated and natural, the expression of this impulse in the act of Christian worship must be

---

[1] George Hedley, *When Protestants Worship* (Nashville: Abingdon Press, 1961), pp. 8-9.

[2] Roger L. Shinn, *The Educational Mission of Our Church* (Philadelphia: United Church Press, 1962), p. 20.

learned. The church properly looks to Christian education to provide this training. Irwin G. Paulsen writes:

> To rear a generation so schooled is dependent on a *curriculum of worship* in the church school, a curriculum that makes conscious and systematic provision for experiences of worship, training in worship, and the relating of the boy and girl at a given age to the common worship of the church with the hope and expectation that the practice will be maintained throughout maturity.[3]

Dr. Paulsen goes on to express the confidence that through such training a church may be built wherein the act of worship has its rightful place, a ministry of which the communicants will avail themselves as a matter of course.

Training cannot effectively be given apart from the actual experience of worship. It grows out of and leads back into this experience. Since teaching is most effective when it takes place in a "natural setting," that is, as guidance and interpretation of an actual experience to which it is related, the fact that Christian education takes place within a worshiping fellowship should make education in worship particularly effective.

WHO SHOULD BE CONCERNED?

The improvement of worship, and worship training, in the church school should be the concern of every worker. While the responsibility rests particularly on those whose work includes conducting worship activities, all who are involved in curriculum are also involved with worship.

Pastors. By training, experience, and task-assignment pastors are most competent and responsible to foster the

---

[3] Irwin G. Paulsen, *The Church School and Worship,* ed. C. A. Bowen (rev. ed.; Nashville: Abingdon Press, 1940), p. 11.

worship life of their congregations. It is the pastor who plans and conducts the general service of his congregation. The effectiveness of any plan for relating the church school to this service depends on his understanding and appreciation of what is intended. Moreover he should be actively concerned with worship in the church school and other groups, through overseeing the whole program, teaching lay leaders of worship, and from time to time conducting worship in these groups.

Committees on Christian Education. By definition of task, such committees are responsible for the nature, content, and direction of the whole curriculum, and this must include a concern for worship. In cooperation with the pastor, such committees are best able to devise and maintain desirable relationships between the church school and the church in general.

Church School Superintendents. The general superintendent is responsible for coordination, direction, and supervision of the whole program, and this includes concern for worship wherever it occurs. He will encourage and guide worship leaders, and help to provide the rooms, equipment, materials, and general conditions which are conducive to worship. In some cases he may himself be expected to lead worship in a department or a combination of departments.

Superintendents or Head Teachers of Departments. Usually these are the persons who are most directly responsible for providing worship and training in worship for the departments to which they are related. In cases where worship is made an integral part of class activity, there may be only occasional department assemblies. However, the department head will still be directly concerned with helping each class achieve its maximum potential in worship.

Class Teachers and Group Leaders. These will in some cases provide for worship in their own groups, and in all cases share in training pupils in worship. By their own conduct, they should be living examples of worshipful participation in services led by others.

Students. In older departments of the church school, youth groups, and adult groups, the students may from time to time be called on to work on worship committees, to share in program leadership, and always to participate intelligently and devotionally as members of the worshiping congregation.

TRAINING FOR LEADERSHIP

To lead others in an experience of worship is a difficult and exacting art. It requires personal qualities of conviction and devotion; an understanding of the nature of worship and the means through which others can best be led into this experience; historical perspective; a sense of fitness and timing; an effective use of voice and personal attitude; the ability to enter sympathetically into the attitudes and feelings of others. There is no more difficult task in Christian education leadership.

Ministers spend many hours of their seminary training in preparation for leadership of public worship. But in the church school we expect laymen to perform this art without previous preparation and little in-service training. It should be no surprise to anyone that this, which should be of the highest quality, is often the most inadequate element in the curriculum. As a consequence we are not developing a generation of Christians who joyously and meaningfully participate in the worship of God in the church. Their attendance is often sporadic, their understanding of what takes place in worship inadequate, and their participation in it ineffective. One does not need to observe many church schools or congregations to be convinced of the truth of these comments.

This is not intended to be an indictment of those who are faithfully trying to do their best as worship leaders in the church school. Most of them are aware of their inadequacies. They want to learn to do better. Some years ago, in preparation for the writing of a book entitled *The Church School*, I asked a large number of superintendents on what problems they would like most to have help. The one request that stood out above all others was for help in leading worship.

There was a disturbing implication in those answers. The request was mostly for materials to use in worship. The assumption seemed to be that anyone can lead worship if he has the necessary prayers, poems, stories, pictures, litanies, and other resources for putting together a service. This is not the place to begin. Effective leadership must begin with an understanding of what worship is, and what constitutes a liturgy. Such materials do have a proper place in an order of worship. Leaders of worship do need help in finding materials that are appropriate. But no combination of elements which have been prepared by someone else will assure effective leadership unless there is understanding of what is being done and why. Conversely any leader who has this understanding will be able to devise or select the appropriate materials. Helps for leaders of worship may be extremely useful, provided that the leader "internalizes" them as his own, and clearly understands their purpose and meaning. Rarely will any leader be able to use a prepared service in toto without adapting it to the needs of the local group and the nature of the occasion.

Can a general book on worship in the church school relate to the needs of worship leaders who are working with pupils of varying ages? It is assumed that this is possible. The nature of worship is basically the same, no matter what the age of the worshiper. The principles underlying an order of worship are the same, though adaptation in form and content is necessary in light of the age and experience of the worshipers.

It is not possible, however, in a general book on worship to give as many resource suggestions as workers with given departments may wish to have. No one book can do this. A leader of worship needs a library—an assortment of books, periodicals, pictures and other visual aids—to which he can turn for resources. Excellent books are available for the guidance of workers in specific departments. Such resources will be indicated at appropriate places. The reader should consider this book as a starting point, and equip himself with additional resources in accordance with his own need.

2 THE MEANING OF WORSHIP

The worship of God is a dominant motif in the life of Christians, and hence the focal point of the life of the church. Oliver Powell has forcefully emphasized "the sheer necessity of being faithful, in season and out, to what is our ultimate business, the worship of God. In a sense, this is *all* we are asked to do, to keep renewing life itself at its roots, at the deep springs of its being. Everything else follows from it."[1]

Anything that is so significant in the life of the individual Christian, and so important to the church, has a priority claim on Christian education, which takes as its task the introducing of persons into the life of the community of Christian faith. Those who would lead others in worship and teach them to understand its meaning must

---

[1] Oliver Powell, *Household of Power* (Philadelphia: United Church Press, 1962), p. 76.

first come to such understanding and experience within themselves.

SOME MISTAKEN IDEAS

It might be assumed that anyone who has grown up in the Christian church will know what worship is. Such is not necessarily the case. Everyone does, of course, have his own ideas, depending on what his experience has been and his reflection on this. But many have thought little about it. Their understanding may be inadequate at best, and grossly mistaken at worst.

In an average congregation there are probably some persons who hold one or more of the following views.

Worship is a more or less meaningless preliminary to the main business of hearing a sermon—an activity that must be endured as a price for the sermon.

There is little or no connection between the sermon and the other elements of the service, with the latter regarded as worship and the former as a separate intellectual and inspirational event.

Worship is a series of formal ritualistic elements that have little conscious meaning for the worshiper, or conversely, worship is an inner experience that has no need of ritual.

Worship is primarily the act of the minister to which the people are passive onlookers except for a few opportunities to join in singing and responses.

The purpose of worship is to win God's favor, so as to assure the good in life and avoid the evil.

Worship is a sort of public entertainment to be enjoyed by the congregation—especially the music and sermon.

Worship is an honored traditional ritual which can be performed by habit.

Worship has no meaning at all (if judgment is made on the basis of such persons' habitual absence or their half attention when present).

If such is the case with the congregation, how is it with those who are church school leaders of worship? What is their understanding of what they are doing when they plan and conduct a service of worship? For some it is little more than putting together some hymns, prayers, poems, music, a story or talk, responses, in some kind of order to make a program, with little purpose other than that this is the way it has always been done. Some think of it as a sort of school assembly, put on for the morale and entertainment of the pupils. Some see it as an opportunity for mass teaching. Some regard its chief value as providing an opportunity for pupil activity, by having them share in planning and conducting the service.

This is not a condemnation of churchgoers or worship leaders, but an attempt at a realistic appraisal of the need which must be met if we are to have better worship in the church school. Let those to whom these statements do not apply rejoice in their better understanding. But let those who feel the need for a greater depth of understanding consider carefully the following venture in interpretation.

WHAT IS WORSHIP?

It is difficult if not impossible to formulate a single statement that embraces the total meaning of worship. Such an effort at capsuling would be likely to capture only a part of the truth, or be so concise as to be incomprehensible. It is better to make a number of statements which describe the characteristics of Christian worship. These taken together may give some understanding of what we are called on to do when ever we assume the role of leading others.

To begin with, a consideration of the meaning of the word itself will be helpful. As a number of writers have pointed out, the word worship is a contraction of an older word, worthship, meaning "to ascribe worth, to hold in honor and esteem." Since there are many things and persons which people hold in high esteem—regard as worthful —a broad implication is that they are objects of worship. Indeed, we speak of men as worshiping wealth, power, possessions, their wives and children, themselves. When this becomes a regard that overtops all others, it is idolatry, replacing God as the object of highest devotion. The word is however more properly and narrowly used to mean the worship of God, and it is this connotation with which we are here concerned.

Worship is not limited to Christians, but is a central element in all religions. Through worship man expresses his esteem for the powers which he conceives to have control over his destiny, and seeks relationship with them or control over them. The form and content are determined by the worshiper's conception of the nature of God (or the gods) and their disposition and responsiveness to him. Primitive man tended to regard his gods as being capricious and vindictive, so his worship consisted of ceremonies and sacrifices through which they might be appeased and their favor incurred. Worship had little relation to man's attitudes and conduct toward his fellowman, since moral conduct was not demanded by the gods either of themselves or their worshipers. Primitive ideas of worship linger on today in some churchgoers, who regard attendance as a duty, and faithfulness in worship as insurance that good will befall them and that evil will be avoided. But this is not Christian worship.

We are concerned with Christian worship. As with all worship, Christian worship is an act which seeks relationship with a supreme being; but when the Christian worships, he seeks communion with God as revealed in Jesus Christ. Through the teaching of the Scriptures, confirmed by his own inner experience, the Christian approaches God in worship in the assurance that:

He is a living God, who created heaven and earth, and sustains his creation with loving concern. He is within the world as well as above it.

He is a mystery, to be approached in wonder and awe, but yet not wholly unknown, for he reveals himself to those who approach him in faith. He is great beyond man's mind to comprehend, but sufficiently revealed to meet man's need.

He is graciously disposed toward man, as a good father to his children—caring, nurturing, admonishing, loving. He is not far off in the heavens, but "nearer than breathing, closer than hands and feet." He seeks us before we seek him, loves us before we love him, gives himself to us before we are ready to give ourselves to him.

He is of supreme worth, to whom alone man's highest worship can be offered.

But this is not all. This same God has made man for himself, and so created him that, through the Holy Spirit, man may enter into relation with him in faith. Hence we may properly speak of worship as communion (or communication) with God, a two-way communication, in which God speaks to those who listen in faith, and hears those who approach him humbly and obediently to worship in spirit and truth.

What, then, is Christian worship? It is man's response to the greatness and goodness of God, his personal act of communion, in which God is addressed and heard. It engages man's whole being, informing and ennobling the mind, exalting the heart, and moving the will to action. In the words of William Temple, "to worship is to quicken the conscience by the holiness of God, to feed the mind by the truth of God, to purge the imagination by the beauty of God, to open the heart to the love of God, to devote the will to the purpose of God."[2] Worship is a service rendered to God, not a self-service in anticipation of some personal benefit. It is the central act of the Christian life, empowering and ennobling all else that constitutes Christian living.

Two analogies may be helpful to further understanding. Robert Seneca Smith has likened the worship of God to human friendship. "If we cultivate a person for what we can get out of him, no real friendship emerges. But if we come to know him just for the sake of fellowship, blessed results follow. They may take a practical and material form. But they are always by-products."[3]

John G. Williams has pointed out that the experience of worship may be compared on the human plane with falling in love. To a person in love, the object of his love is of supreme worth, occupies his constant thoughts, and determines all his activities.

> It inflames him with a desire to be his best in everything; to please, honor, and serve the beloved. . . . There is no single aspect of his daily life, however trivial, that is not touched and empowered and enriched by it. That is a glimpse of what it means to worship God. There is a sense in which religion means being in love with God. . . . Once

---

[2] William Temple, *The Hope of a New World* (New York: Macmillan, 1942), p. 30.

[3] Robert Seneca Smith, *The Art of Group Worship* (Nashville: Abingdon Press, 1938), p. 23.

see God as the one truly "worthwhile" object of our thoughts, love, and energy and then every conceivable detail of life—home, work, recreation, friendships, aims and ideals —will be permeated by one all-embracing purpose, to please and honor God.[4]

WHY WORSHIP?

Why do we worship? Because we are so constituted that we must; we cannot do otherwise. We eat because we cannot live without food. We communicate with others because we cannot exist as persons apart from human relationships. We worship because our very existence demands that we give our devotion to Something outside ourselves; our religious nature demands that we find meaning for our existence in a Supreme Being.

The motivation to worship is supported by a number of urges that arise from our nature as human creatures: Awe and wonder in the presence of God's greatness and goodness dispose us to respond with reverence and adoration. Consciousness of inadequacy, unworthiness, and sin lead us to confession and the desire for forgiveness and acceptance. Gratitude for his unspeakable gift of himself, for his "redemption of the world by our Lord Jesus Christ," and for all his "goodness and loving-kindness to us and to all men" leads us to offer "most humble and hearty thanks."[5] Our sense of continuing need and our concern for the need of others make us bold to ask for renewed and new blessings, including that of a fuller self-

---

[4] John G. Williams, *Worship and the Modern Child* (London: National Society, S.P.C.K., 1957), pp. 9-10.

[5] From the prayer of General Thanksgiving, *The Book of Common Prayer*.

revelation of God and his will through the hearing of his word in scripture and sermon. Our faith in his wisdom, which is infinitely above our own, impels us, in reverent obedience and submission, to pray that not our wills but his be done and that he will direct our lives and use our efforts. These elements—adoration, confession, thanksgiving, supplication, submission—are all present in the complete act of prayer and worship, though one or another of them may dominate at times.[6]

What Happens When We Worship? We turn our minds and hearts to God, and give him the love, honor, and praise which are his due. We commune with God, and affirm our life in him—in him we live and move and are (Acts 17:28). This is the heart of the matter. We do not presume to change God, for he is unchangeable. But by our attitude toward him we open channels for his grace toward us. On our part, we experience joy and exaltation because we have been in God's presence; a renewed perspective on life; assurance that he is with us in our deepest needs and aspirations, if our desires are in harmony with his will; confidence and strength for our daily task; a resolve so to live "that we may show forth thy praise, not only with our lips, but in our lives, by giving up ourselves to thy service, and by walking before thee in holiness and righteousness all our days."[7]

These motives, and the possibility for these experiences, are not limited to mature men and women. They are pres-

---

[6] One of my teachers once made a suggestion that has been very helpful to me. To remember these five elements in prayer and worship, think of the word Acts spelled with double *s*, made up of the initial letters of these words, thus: A—adoration, C—confession, T—thanksgiving, S—supplication, S—submission.

[7] Prayer of General Thanksgiving, *The Book of Common Prayer*.

ent in some degree at all ages. The experience of worship is as real for the young child as for the mature adult, though the forms and words through which it comes to expression are to some extent conditioned by the age of the worshiper.

There may be those who say that such an experience of worship rarely comes to them. Let it be admitted that perhaps few of us ever fully attain it. But to understand what may take place in worship is a long step toward achievement. In a sense there is little we can do about it. The ability to worship is a gift from God, by grace of the Holy Spirit. Nevertheless God's action requires a readiness on man's part to respond. When we attend a service which "leaves us cold," without a sense of having worshiped, it is not that God is not present and responsive, but rather that we are not in a seeking and responsive mood. The fault with some is that they expect an experience without any effort on their part. Worship requires active participation, perseverance, and discipline.

Some judge the reality of worship by the intensity of their emotional experience. This is a mistaken criterion. Worship is an offering of the whole being—body and mind and soul—and is not dependent on a particular emotional reaction. This is not to say that the emotions are not involved. True worship must be from the heart—sincere, unfeigned—and such an act cannot be performed without some feeling about it, but the emotion is secondary to the act.

WORSHIP IN THE CHURCH

In considering the meaning of worship, we have not distinguished sharply between worship in general and worship as a scheduled activity in the church. When we think of worship as an experience which is not scheduled in any particular time or place, we can probably maintain that it is something which most people do at one time or other. It is a spontaneous activity that may happen at any time and is not dependent on presence in a church service.

It is worship as an activity of the Christian church with which we are primarily concerned. Let us change our question, then, from "Why do we worship?" to: "Why do people attend church for divine worship?" This is not the same as asking why people attend church, for they may have numerous reasons other than participation in worship. What is the motive that brings people together week after week for the worship of God? If they could put their reasons into words—which many probably cannot—the answers might run something like this: We need a time and place that are set aside for deliberate attention to our relation to God. We know that just as nibbling does not take the place of proper eating, and casual contacts, the place of satisfying association with friends, so unplanned flashes of worship do not take the place of proper communion with God. We need the ordered liturgy of the church as a vehicle through which to express our impulse to worship. We need the nurture and discipline in the meaning and practice of worship that attendance at church provides. We need the strength and support that come through fellowship with other Christians in worship.

It is only fair to ask the question in reverse also: Why do some people *not* attend worship in the church? While it may be true that there are few people who do not at times worship, it is an obvious fact that there are many who attend church irregularly or not at all. If they were to speak, and speak honestly, their answers might go something like this: We do not have a sufficient sense of the reality of God in our lives to impel us to attend formal worship. Our conception of God is not such as to elicit our worship. We do not find the church service helpful. We are quite able to take care of ourselves and do not need any help from God. We try to live honestly and decently, so what more is there to religion?

Such negative attitudes toward worship in the church are due to faulty Christian education, at least in part. Many of these people were at one time in our church schools. They were in many cases confirmed by the church. Just as the disciples asked Jesus, "Lord, teach us to pray," so they were asking, "Church, teach us to worship." But somehow we failed them. Their innate impulses toward the worship of God were scarcely different from those of their fellow pupils who now make public worship a regular part of their lives. But the church school did not succeed in nurturing and channeling those impulses into full participation in the life of the community of faith. This is the challenge to all who are working in Christian education: to make renewed effort to strengthen that part of the church's teaching program which has to do with the nurture of the worship life.

Why Does a Church Have Worship? The answer to this question may be summarized in a few brief statements which follow from our prior discussion:

1. The church conducts worship because it is inherent in her very nature to do so.

Obviously the single most important thing a church does in a given week is to gather its people for the public worship of God. In one sense it is the *only* important thing it does, for from that stems everything else. In worship everything is seen in true perspective. Without it . . . a church becomes merely one more society of earnest, conscientious people eager to do the right thing, but in danger of living truncated and trivial lives.[8]

2. Public worship provides an opportunity in an appropriate place, with a carefully prepared liturgy, for God's people to gather for the corporate act which is the highest expression of the Christian life. It gives tone and direction to the expressions of worship which may occur more spontaneously and informally in the home and at other points in daily life throughout the week.

3. Worship is essential because the church is in constant need of the renewal of her life if she is not to lose sight of her ultimate reason for being and slip into complacent self-satisfaction and mere busyness. John Heuss has expressed this in these words: "I firmly believe that every effort a local parish makes to increase the meaningfulness of its worship and prayer life will do more than anything else to restore that parish to its true religious function."[9] The church has an essential mission which exists and comes to reality through its members as they are scattered to every part of the world in their daily round of activity. To enable them to engage in this mission it is necessary that they also come together for renewal of perspective and energy in the ministry of worship.

4. Worship is a corporate act of the gathered congregation, and something more than a collection of individuals, each saying his private prayers. True, the congregation consists of individual worshipers, but when the liturgy is the expression of the whole congregation, it becomes more

---

[8] Powell, *op. cit.*, pp. 87-88.

[9] John Heuss, *Our Christian Vocation* (New York: Seabury Press, 1955), p. 13.

31

than the sum of its individual elements. When a congregation engages in Christian worship it is the people of God making an approach to God.

Why Have Worship in the Church School? Is it not sufficient to have a general service for the whole congregation?

One reason commonly given is that the general service is of necessity pitched at a level of maturity which is beyond the comprehension of children; hence something similar should be provided for them—a sort of "children's church." There is truth in this contention. Corporate worship does have elements that are difficult for children, but it is not wholly incomprehensible to them. As with any participation in family or community life, it is an experience they will grow up to by participation within it. To deprive children of any part in corporate worship is to neglect an important element in their Christian education.

Nevertheless worship in the church school is an essential part of the curriculum, for the following reasons:

1. There is a total worship life of the church which includes many occasions and groups besides the Sunday morning congregation. The classes and departments of the church school are such groups. It is fitting that they should include worship as a part of their activity. Nor is this something which is just *added to* teaching. It illuminates and gives perspective to all that is done, and serves to make it *Christian* education.

2. Whatever may be their participation in the corporate worship of the church, younger members should have an opportunity to participate in worship which is more within their experience, vocabulary, and attention span, and uses materials which are more within their comprehension, than is the case in a general service.

3. The church school takes responsibility for education in worship as well as for experience of it. In fact the two are inseparably related. The church school relates two factors that are important in effective learning—experience, and instruction in the meaning of that experience. From simple beginnings children will progress to everincreasing ability and understanding toward lifelong participation in the corporate worship of the congregation. In this connection a caution needs to be voiced: In their zeal for education, leaders should not use worship simply as an instrument for demonstration and teaching. The primary purpose must always be sincere worship, but this does not prevent having by-products in learning.

3   ORDERS OF WORSHIP

Group worship is a scheduled activity that takes place at an appointed time for a period varying from a few minutes to an hour. It involves activities of a leader and the congregation through which they seek to come into relationship with God—a two-way communication from God to people and from people to God. Those who plan and conduct worship need to find and use the best means through which this communication may become a reality. This requires both content and form, appropriate events in a proper setting. It includes hearing, seeing, and doing—hearing God's word and will in scripture and sermon, receiving and giving communication through music and symbolic objects and acts, joining in prayer, song, responses, and giving.

DESIGN FOR WORSHIP

The sequence of planned events for a service of worship constitutes the *order of worship* or *liturgy*. It is a formal pattern of speaking and listening, hearing and seeing, meditative silence and overt activity, through which God may act and the people respond. "Liturgy" means literally "the work of the people" in praising God and seeking refreshment and renewal of their spiritual lives, and committing themselves to him. The several elements of the liturgy constitute the *ritual*. Worship is more than a matter of engaging in the words and acts of the ritual. These are but an outward expression of an "inner and spiritual grace."

Corporate worship engages the active participation of the whole congregation. It is not something a leader does to which the people are passive witnesses. This is significantly expressed in the meaning of the word liturgy as the work of the people. Those who would experience worship should heed the admonition and trust the promise in Deuteronomy 4:29: "Seek the Lord your God, and you will find him, if you search after him with all your heart and with all your soul."

The need for this condition of active involvement on the part of the worshiper has been forcefully put by Sören Kierkegaard in an essay on "The Listener's Role in a Devotional Address." He says that if the talk is to be helpful to you, it will be the result of your own activity—that *you* will be the one to whom and for whom the word is spoken. It does not depend on the speaker's artistry or eloquence. Although this may be helpful, it is not the essence. Eloquence is a frill—like beauty, it is helpful, but not essential. The essential characteristic is earnestness on the part of the listener.[1]

With this interpretation, the common designation which we use for corporate worship as a "service of worship" is

---

[1] Sören Kierkegaard, *Purity of Heart Is to Will One Thing*, trans. Douglas V. Steere. (New York: Harper & Bros., 1938), ch. 12.

appropriate. It is an offering to God of ourselves in his praise, in thanksgiving, and in dedication to him. Without pressing the distinction too far, we may think of the order of worship as the planned program through which a congregation may be enabled to receive the blessing of an experience in the presence of God, while liturgy (or the service of worship) is their participation in the acts of worship which are set forth in the order.

CONTENT OF WORSHIP

Liturgy is concerned with the true ordering of the church's service to God. Ritual deals only with the details of those actions which attempt to be the appropriate outward expression of the church's liturgy. They deserve some attention but unless they are kept firmly in their subordinate place they can cause the church to lose sight of the true purpose of its worship.[2]

What are the activities which constitute a service of worship, and how should they be put together in a proper "order"? "A good order of worship is one that leads us into the presence of God without calling undue attention to itself, or requiring too much concentration on what comes next."[3] Anything which contributes to worship may have a place in a service. Tradition and experience have established certain elements as most appropriate, and these will be commonly used. In planning a service, the selection of elements will be made by the criterion: What will best help this congregation to worship? Any other questions—

---

[2] Daniel Jenkins, *The Protestant Ministry* (Garden City, N. Y.: Doubleday, 1958), p. 47.

[3] Frank M. Weiskel, "Worship—How to? or Whom to?" *Helping Children Worship* (Philadelphia: United Church Board for Homeland Ministries, Division of Christian Education, n.d.) p. 11.

Is this interesting? Is this familiar? Will they like this?—
are secondary to the main purpose. Following are the elements most commonly used:

Hymns. "Make a joyful noise to God, all the earth; sing
the glory of his name; give to him glorious praise!" (Ps.
66:1-2) This is a call to sing, and singing is almost always
a part of worship.

> A Christian hymn is a lyric poem, devotional in spirit and
> reverent in tone, which is designed to be sung and which ex-
> presses the worshiper's attitude toward God, or God's pur-
> pose in human life. It should be simple and metrical in
> form, genuinely emotional and literary in style, spiritual in
> quality, and in its ideas so direct and immediately apparent
> as to unify a congregation singing it.[4]

The hymnal constitutes a great resource of materials
through which we may praise God and pray to him, celebrate his nature and attributes, express our sense of sin
and hope of redemption, voice our aspirations for the
Christian life.

A hymn consists of words and music, appropriately wed-
ded to achieve a single intellectual and emotional experience. The words are of primary importance and should be
understood and consciously made our own if singing is to
be with heart and mind as well as with voice. The tune is
a help in expressing the sentiment of the words, and may
serve to establish an emotional experience which is re-
created at each subsequent use. When people say that they
love certain hymns it is probably because rich associations

---

[4] Carl F. Price, *Paper VI:* "What Is a Hymn?" (New York: The Hymn
Society of America, 1937).

have been built up around them, but the love should be for both the words and the music.

Hymns should be selected for quality, appropriateness to the particular service, and suitability for the age-group. The words should be good poetry and reasonably within the experience and understanding of the worshipers. The music should be appropriate to the sentiment of the words and within the capacity of the pupils to sing. If a good hymnbook is used, one that has been prepared for the department in question, most of the hymns will be suitable for that age.

Normally all the stanzas of a hymn will be sung at each use, and some hymns require all the stanzas to give their complete thought. Omission of stanzas should not be made at random, lest this result in distortion of meaning or discontinuity in line of thought. I recall being present in a service in which "The First Noel" was used, and the leader announced that only the first four stanzas would be sung. But the five stanzas of this hymn tell a continuous story of which the fifth is the climax. This is an instance of the common practice of some leaders to give little thought to the words and meaning of hymns. Two conditions may make it desirable to omit one or more stanzas: (1) if they are not suitable for the group or for the particular occasion; (2) if the limitation of time makes it necessary. In the latter case the leader should make a study of all the stanzas before deciding which may best be omitted.

Prayer. Prayer is an essential element and the high point in worship. It is present at many points in the liturgy—invocation, confession, some hymns and scripture readings, litanies and other responses, dedication of the offering, benediction, and particularly in the pastoral or general prayer. Other parts of the service may be about God and our relation to him, but prayer is conversation with God himself.

Prayer is addressed to God, in faith that he will hear and respond. It is not a lecture to God or the congregation. It is not an occasion for moral admonitions, addressed to the congregation through God in support of the exhortation in the sermon. It is little short of blasphemy to use prayer simply as a means of teaching and admonishing the worshipers. Prayer is communion with God.

Leading a group in prayer is the most difficult part of conducting worship. It is an art that requires facilitating the whole worshiping group to come into the presence of God in praise and supplication. The leader must be so sensitive to their needs and longings that he can unify them in expressing these in words appropriate to prayer. The words used in prayer should be beautiful and dignified and at the same time also simple and common to the language and mode of expression of the worshipers. Hackneyed words and pious phrases which signify nothing should be avoided. The voice should be natural and sincere, with no trace of sanctimoniousness. This applies to leaders of all groups, but most particularly to those who are privileged to lead the worship of children. The leader should be sure that he, with the congregation, is praying to God, not addressing the congregation.

What should be included in prayer? The simplest way to answer this is to refer to the elements in the act of worship given on page 27, which come to clearest focus in prayer—adoration, confession, thanksgiving, supplication, submission. If the leader has these in mind, remembering that they are responses to common needs of all who pray, he will be able to articulate a prayer that avoids the merry-

go-round of "God bless this and that" which is so common
in church school prayers. This is not to say that he is to
dwell at length on each of these elements in every prayer,
or even that all should be present in every prayer. Brevity,
conciseness, and simplicity are virtues in any prayer, and
particularly in prayers with children, whose attention span
is brief. On this point, Robert Seneca Smith has suggested:

> The writer believes that prayers should be brief. It is im-
> possible for the mind to dwell long on any theme. One
> would do well to study the form of the collect in the *Book
> of Common Prayer,* and observe how much is said in the
> briefest compass. "Almighty God, unto whom all hearts are
> open, all desires known, and from whom no secrets are hid:
> cleanse the thoughts of our hearts by the inspiration of thy
> Holy Spirit, that we may perfectly love thee and worthily
> magnify thy holy name. Through Jesus Christ our Lord.
> Amen." That is a perfect prayer both in content and form.[5]

Careful preparation is necessary for leadership in prayer.
If a prayer is to be selected from a book of worship or
other source, the appropriate one must be found and so
internalized that it becomes the leader's own. If it is to be
of the leader's own composition, as is usually the case with
the pastoral prayer, it must be carefully planned in advance, and preferably written. Writing a prayer is helpful,
whether the text is to be read or is to serve as a guide in
extemporaneous expression. No general rule can be made
as to whether prayers should be read or freely spoken.
Some prefer to read the prayer; others feel that it has more
reality when spoken without the limitations of a written
text. Each must do that which best enables him to unify

---

[5] Robert Seneca Smith, *The Art of Group Worship* (Nashville: Abingdon
Press, 1938), p. 76.

the group in common prayer. If pupils are to lead in prayer, it is especially important that they be helped in preparation, and if a prayer is written for them, that it be in thoughts and words which are their own.

Scripture Readings. Readings and recitations from the Bible have an essential place in the service of worship. The Bible is a record of God's relation to man, of God's activity and promises and man's response. It is God's word to man, revealed in history, story, prophecy, biography, sermon, psalm, and other forms.

> The Bible . . . is the norm by which the church must test its faithfulness to the mission it has been given to proclaim the gospel. Read and interpreted within the church, it is, so to speak, the rendezvous which God has chosen for meeting and speaking with man, the "holy ground" on which God confronts man with his humbling and forgiving word.[6]

When we seek communion with God it is natural that the Bible should be used as a unique means for achieving this purpose. Such values, however, do not result from casual selection and careless reading, with little purpose other than that Bible reading is expected to be included in a service of worship. Selection of readings must be made with careful thought to filling a unique place in the total design of the service, and read with such sincerity and conviction that God's word may be heard through the voice of the leader.

The Bible has a proper place at many points in worship —calls to worship and benedictions, responses, invitation to giving, the basis (text) for the sermon or other message,

---

[6] Bernhard W. Anderson, "The Bible," *A Handbook of Christian Theology*, eds. Marvin Halverson and Arthur A. Cohen (Cleveland: Meridian Books, World Publishing Co., 1958), p. 35.

the content of many hymns, the symbolism of the open Bible, and especially the reading of a passage for the "lesson" of the day.

The reading of the Bible is an ancient and continuing practice in Christian worship. It probably was a more climactic event in days when Bibles were not available to the people. The fact that almost every Christian now has his own Bible might cause us to wonder whether public reading is still necessary. But having the Bible and using it are quite different matters. It is a safe guess that for most worshipers the reading and study of the Bible is limited to their experience with it in the church. In any case this question is beside the point. The purpose of using the Bible in worship is not that the worshiper may gain greater familiarity with its content, although this should be a desirable by-product. It is used so that each may hear anew God's word to him and so that he may respond to it in the present encounter.

The Bible selection may be read by the leader or the congregation may share in reading responsively or in unison. Whatever may be the value of responsive reading for a mature congregation, I question its usefulness in the worship of children. It is not conducive to getting the sense of a whole passage to have it read responsively. Instead of giving attention to the parts read by the leader, children will as likely as not be looking ahead to what they are to read next. It would therefore seem better to read in unison when it is desired that the congregation participate in the reading.

How should the passage for reading be selected? Since there are no lectionaries that suggest appropriate selections for each Sunday in the departments of the church school, the choice must be made by the one who prepares the service. In general the reading should be of a nature appropriate to use in worship. Not all parts of the Bible are equally suitable. The selection should be appropriate also for the age of the worshiping group. More particularly, the reading in any service should usually be such that it serves either as a basis for the central theme of the service or helps to illuminate and reinforce it. The selection should not be overly long. In the case of young children, a single verse may best serve the purpose. While it is not customary for the minister to do this in a general congregational service, for church school groups it may at times be helpful for the leader to introduce the reading with a brief interpretation of its setting and significance so as to make it more meaningful.

As with prayer, the reading of the Bible should be an experience of the whole group. Participation of pupils will be in the form of attentively listening as the leader reads, silently following the reading in their own Bibles if they come equipped with them, or joining in unison reading or recitation. If a pupil is to serve as the reader, he should be coached in doing this properly. It is not an opportunity to show off, but to lead others in worship. Choral readings may be used with good effect if care is taken that they will enhance worship and not simply be a presentation for the enjoyment of the congregation.

Sermon. A service of worship will usually include a spoken message by the leader. In the worship of younger groups we do not usually call this a "sermon" or "preaching" but it has essentially the same purpose as the sermon in general worship. This purpose is to proclaim the grace, love, mercy, judgment, and will of God to the minds and hearts of the worshipers. Their response should be to God, not to the preacher. The sermon will usually instruct the learners so that they will better understand the meaning of their life with God, but it is more than teaching. It appeals to the emotions and the will as well as to the mind. It is a witness to the preacher's own faith, serving to encourage, counsel, and inspire the hearers in their faith. It will normally have a close relation to the Bible reading. "And they read from the book, from the law of God, clearly; and they gave the sense, so that the people understood the reading" (Neh. 8:8).

With particular reference to the church school: the sermon serves to interpret, illumine, and reinforce the theme of the whole service. It may be a discourse, a story, a visual presentation, a dramatization, or a combination of discourse with one of the other forms. With younger children the sermon is more often in the form of a story. This is good practice provided that the story is appropriate to the theme, brief, well told, and not used simply as a vehicle for moral admonition at the end. It is my experience that a discourse-type of presentation can be effectively used even with young children. In such case particular attention must be given to concrete rather than abstract content, and to simple words, short sentences, and brevity. A few simple sentences will often serve the purpose.

A problem of peculiar difficulty is encountered when the leader must address his sermon—or for that matter plan a whole service—to a congregation of widely varying ages, as in a family service. This will be considered in chapter 4.

Responses. A liberal use of responses by the pupils helps to enrich the service and involves them more fully in it. Appropriate sentences (usually scriptural passages) may be used for the call to worship, call to prayer (for example,

"The Lord be with you. . . . And with thy spirit"), call to giving, benediction. It is one purpose of memory work to have pupils commit such verses to memory so that they can freely respond at the appointed times. Such responses can also be facilitated by having copies of the order of service in the hands of pupils.

A comment is in order concerning the use of "Amen" at the end of hymns and prayers. Most pupils, if they think about it at all, probably regard this simply as a customary way of ending a religious utterance, like a period at the end of a sentence. From occasional use of the word in ordinary conversation they may know that it means agreement with and strong affirmation of a statement that has been made. Someone has suggested that its meaning may be likened to our colloquial expression "You can say that again!" What they need to learn is that "Amen" has a positive place and meaning in liturgy. It is a declaration that there is agreement with and acceptance of what someone else has said or written—making it one's own sentiment. Taken seriously, such use of the word would require that the worshiper give close attention to the sense of the words of hymns, prayers, and responses which he will affirm with his own "Amen." This may be a small matter, but it is one that too often has been neglected in education for worship.

I have always liked the custom in some congregations of having the people join with the minister in audibly speaking the "Amen" at the end of a prayer. It would, I think, be helpful to teach pupils to do so, with understanding of what it means.

Offering. The giving of money has an appropriate place in worship. It has a desirable place in church school wor-

45

ship, and also helps to accustom pupils to this practice in the church service. It provides an opportunity for education in the meaning of Christian stewardship. Most pupils appreciate being permitted to take turns in taking the offering and can be trained to do this in proper form and with dignity.

The use of offering envelopes is desirable for training in regular and systematic giving. It also has the practical value of avoiding having coins accidentally dropped on the floor and rolling out of reach. Pupils should learn that they are making their offering to the whole church and its causes, not just to the church school. Hence it is wise for them to have the same type of envelope used in the adult congregation, not a juvenile version of it for use in the church school.

Since younger children may have difficulty in holding their offering until the time of collection, or finding it at that time, offering baskets or plates may be placed at the door so that the offering can be deposited on arrival. When the time for the offering is reached in the service, the appointed "deacons" will simply bring the baskets or plates forward for dedication rather than at that time collecting from the pupils.

With respect to the appropriate place for the offering in the order of service, it is suggested that this be near the conclusion, so that it may be a symbolic act of response and dedication.

Ceremonials. We have a language of actions as well as a language of words. By ceremonials we mean certain acts and ways of doing things that have symbolic meaning. In common life we call this etiquette—forms in our relations with others which express courtesy, respect, deference, regard, and so forth (the handshake, addressing an older person as "sir," rising when an older person or a lady comes into the room). In international relations we call it protocol—a system of regulations which govern the treatment of the representatives of one government by those of another.

In worship we observe certain forms which help to give enrichment and meaning. On entering the sanctuary, we may sit for a moment of silence and prayer; we may light candles at the opening and extinguish them at the closing of worship; we may stand to sing; we may sit, stand, or kneel for prayer, with bowed head and folded hands as a sign of humility; we try to heed the admonition: "Let all the earth keep silence before him." Education in worship will include an interpretation of the meaning of these ceremonials, and training in the observance of them.

Music. One of the ways in which people express their deepest feelings is through music. Hence music should have a significant place in worship. A good pianist or organist is as important to the service as a good liturgist.

> The church should do more than make us think. It should develop our finer feelings, tastes, and preferences. To do this it must call in the help of art. Music is an art, and church music has been found through the centuries to be one of the best means of cultivating the better emotions of man.[7]

These are the more usual elements which in proper arrangement make up the service of worship. In a non-prescribed liturgy, the leader may use considerable freedom in deciding which elements are to be included and the order in which they are to be arranged. In any case he

---

[7] Charles E. McKinley, *The Meaning of the Church Service* (New York: Congregational Christian Churches, n.d.), p. 24.

must choose the content most appropriate to each service—hymns, scripture, responses, prayer, sermon. Since both form and content vary with the age of the worshipers, we will at this point not give a suggested order. Chapters 8, 9, and 10 deal with specific age-groups.

GENERAL CHARACTER AND QUALITY

What should be true of all Christian education is especially true of worship: nothing but the best is good enough. There are some general qualities which apply to every service, and which leaders may find helpful in checking their work.

1. It is preceded by *preparation*: (a) by the leader in designing the service and selecting the content, and in personally achieving a quiet and devotional mood which is appropriate to this ministry; (b) of the congregation, so that they may be in a mood to approach worship in quiet anticipation of God's presence and blessing.

2. It is *directed to God,* and gives the worshiper an opportunity for communion with him. It avoids everything that is extraneous to or interferes with this purpose.

3. It is *Christian,* with hymns, prayers, story, and other elements so selected as to express and contribute to our highest conception of God in Christ.

4. It is *serious in purpose,* seriously and sincerely conducted by the leader, and eliciting a serious and sincere attitude and response from the congregation.

5. It has *reality,* not a mere speaking of words but an experience of the soul in communion with God.

6. It has *unity*—a central theme, with hymns, scripture, prayer, and sermon contributing to that theme.

7. It has *design* and *movement*: (a) design in providing for the response of adoration, confession, thanksgiving, sup-

plication, and submission-dedication (see p. 27); (b) movement in proceeding from the people's approach to God, to hearing his word and promises in scripture and sermon, to self-dedication.

8. It has *rhythm*, achieved in such ways as through responses between leader and congregation, and through centering attention now on man and his need and again on God and his power and grace to meet that need. "As the service provides opportunity for adoration and confession, for thanksgiving and supplication, for dedication and submission, thus making answer to the elemental urges of the human spirit, one discovers in these changes of mood a certain rhythmic alternation."[8]

9. It is *graded,* that is, properly designed in form and content for the age of the members of the congregation. In case of a wide age range, an effort will be made to select some elements that are within the field of experience of younger members as well as of those who are more mature.

10. There is *participation* by the congregation—outwardly in singing, responses, and offering; inwardly by sharing in the thought of the scripture, prayers, and sermon.

---

[8] Smith, *op. cit.*, p. 36.

4 MAKING PROVISION FOR WORSHIP

Worship is so natural and intimate a factor in Christian education that it may take place at almost any point in the church school program. We are concerned, however, with the planned occasions for worship which are provided in the schedule. While our thought is directed mainly to the Sunday morning program, much of what follows will apply also to worship in various through-the-week groups.

There are three principal ways in which worship may be provided in the curriculum of Christian education: (1) through participation in the common worship of the congregation; (2) in departments of the church school; (3) as an integral part of class sessions. These are not mutually exclusive, and more than one may be included on a given Sunday, or the plan may vary from Sunday to Sunday. It is suggested, however, that on any Sunday the emphasis be on only one as the principal experience in group worship.

THE CHURCH INCLUDES CHILDREN

The highest point in the spiritual life of the church is the weekly gathering of the whole congregation for the worship of God. This is not a service for adults only but for all who are a part of the church fellowship. "The ideal of Christian worship . . . is a community, a true family of young and old, offering their praise to God in unison."[1]

"Worship is the offering to God of the entire congregation of his people, and children should certainly be included. A childless congregation presents an abnormal and an unpromising appearance; and this one sees all too often."[2] No person because of his youth should be deprived of this experience. Christian education, which seeks to introduce persons into the Christian fellowship, must of necessity come to terms with its relationship to common worship.

This presented no problem for our ancestors with whom attendance at both Sunday school and church was a normal expectation for the whole family. This situation still prevails in some churches. It is increasingly common, however, for congregations to consist largely of adults and young people, while children and their teachers attend church school only. There are many causes that are responsible for this change:

1. The growing recognition that the church school *is* the church and not simply a vestibule or adjunct to it, and the enrichment of worship in church school departments,

---

[1] John G. Williams, *Worship and the Modern Child* (London: National Society, S.P.C.K., 1957), p. 129.

[2] Henry Sloane Coffin, *The Public Worship of God* (Philadelphia: Westminster Press, 1946), copyright by W. L. Jenkins, p. 156. Used by permission.

have led to the conclusion that children who are in the church school do not need to attend church.

2. The fact that church services are so generally conducted on the level of adult interest, experience, attention span, and comprehension has brought into question the desirability of expecting children to attend. This represents a gain in behalf of the rights of children, but is a negative answer to the problem.

3. Since it is the nature of children to act as children, particularly when what is going on ignores their understanding and abilities, their presence in the congregation may be a disturbing element for other worshipers. It is not a satisfactory solution to arrange the service wholly at the level of children's comprehension.

4. In case the congregation is scattered over a wide geographical area and parents do not participate in the church school, they may insist on the convenience of having the church school parallel with the church service, thus avoiding having to bring their children at another hour.

5. The same situation results when because of crowded conditions (including congested parking space) the church is forced to conduct two or more services on Sunday morning with parallel church schools. In either case, children and their teachers will by design be in church school while parents and other adults attend the church service. To be sure, in the latter case they could attend church at one of the other hours when they are not in church school, but few will accept this addition of time to their church activity.

6. In many churches there are few parents who desire to enroll in adult church school classes, hence find it a convenience for their children to be in church school while they attend morning worship. This probably increases the

number of adults attending church, but depresses still more the interest in adult study and also makes it more difficult to enlist church school teachers.

We are due for a reconsideration of the relationship between the church and the church school. The segregation that results from choice of one *or* the other is not satisfactory. Nor are the desired results achieved when children are marshaled into an adult service which largely ignores their presence. If Christian education is to be vitally related to corporate worship, more is needed than church attendance by church school pupils, laudable as this may be. Mere attendance does not necessarily establish lifelong habits. True, many of our most faithful church men and women will testify that as children they became accustomed to the habit of church attendance. But there are, no doubt, as many and more who were conditioned against the church because they were required to do what for them held no interest and resulted only in intolerable boredom.

Three conditions must be met if church attendance is to be a vital factor in the Christian education of children: (a) the children should be accepted by the congregation wholeheartedly as fellow worshipers, and not just tolerated; (b) the service—or that part of it which they attend—must be sufficiently within their comprehension and experience to enable them to participate meaningfully; (c) training in the meaning and content of the service should be related to the actual experience so that they may be growing in understanding and appreciation.

Ministers need to be sensitive to the needs of whole families in planning worship. This is not an impossible task for there are many elements in the liturgy which are in the range of children's capacity to participate, especially when their Christian education includes training in worship. Nor is it necessary for all that goes on to be within the comprehension of younger members of the congregation. Children are accustomed to being part of a family in which some conversations and activities are "above their heads." It is a challenge to them to reach up into adult experience as far as they are able, and often their grasp goes beyond our expectations. Church worship is one of the few activities outside the home in which whole families can share together, and the fact that it is something which a family does together probably has enriching value.

There are in fact few elements in the liturgy in which children cannot share with understanding and meaning, when they are given the necessary help. It is the sermon which presents the greatest difficulty because when it is suitable in length and intellectual content for mature persons it is beyond the attention span and comprehension of children. Some ministers manage to preach sermons which at some points catch and hold the interest of younger persons, and this should be attempted when there are children present. But always to be under this necessity is to run into the danger of "watering down" the content for those who need stronger theological stimulation. One way of meeting this problem is to have children leave the service for other activities during the hymn before the sermon. Another way is to have a short story or talk especially for children.

Opinions differ concerning the desirability of having a sermon directed specifically to children. It is good for children to know their minister in his role of preaching, directed to them. If it is well done this may be very effective. Some ministers succeed so well that even adults say they get more from the children's sermon than from the one directed to them (if this is true, it is hardly a compliment for the general preaching).

On the other side are such arguments as: The children's sermon interrupts the design and flow of the liturgy. It may make the service unduly long. It suggests to children that the general sermon is not for them and makes it hard to justify asking them to remain for it. It suggests to the minister that he has fulfilled his obligation to the children and can now forget their presence. Few ministers have mastered the art of preaching to children, so children's sermons may not be relevant to their need in either thought or language, and may be used to "hit" the adults through the children, or descend to the level of a few moralistic admonitions or an inane and insipid secular story. (But why, if the minister considers the children in his congregation an important part of his ministry, should he not school himself to learn how to communicate with them on a meaningful religious level?)

The foregoing discussion has dealt only with the place of children in the congregation. I have assumed that beyond the age of childhood, participation in the congregation at worship is a regular part of church experience.

PATTERNS FOR FAMILY SERVICES

If a case has been made for a close relationship between the church school and the church service, for having pupils of all ages participate in corporate worship, it remains to suggest ways in which this may be worked out. There are a number of patterns by which this may be accomplished and any church that is seriously concerned should be able to find its own best plan. I will suggest three types of plans which are most commonly used.

1. Everyone attends both the church school and the

church service. In churches where this is already the practice (or at least the expectation) no change in pattern is needed. But in order to achieve the greatest values, two steps should be considered: (a) finding ways of making the service meaningful to all ages; (b) so interrelating the church and the church school that they will constitute one unified program, and the church school will contribute adequate training for participation in and appreciation of the service of corporate worship.

2. Younger members of the church school attend the first part of the church service and withdraw for other activities at some point before the sermon. Thus they will be present for that part of the liturgy which is most within the range of their participation, and engage in activities that are appropriate for them during the remainder of the hour. To be of greatest value there should be education of the children in the meaning of the service and education for participation in the hymns and other elements in the liturgy. Church ushers should be instructed to extend the same courtesies to children as to adults, which includes giving copies of the order of service to those who are able to use it.

Since the church offering is usually taken while the children are present, it is best for them also to give their contributions at this time. This presents no administrative problem if offering envelopes are used with a certain range of numbers assigned to church school pupils so that they can easily be separated for accounting. It is an effective way of emphasizing that all offerings are for the work of God's kingdom through the church, not for a separate institution called the church school.

It may be objected that the coming and going of children, and the mere fact of their presence, is a disturbing element which interferes with worship. There may be a measure of truth in this, but the objection is not valid if children are accepted as a part of the Christian fellowship with an inherent right to participate in the worship of the fellowship. Moreover such disturbance can be reduced to a minimum by careful planning, and by training of the children. For example, if the exit is made while the congregation is standing for a hymn, it may happen so unobtrusively as to be scarcely noticed.

This plan has the possibility of many variations. Attendance may be on an every-Sunday basis or only on occasional Sundays. It may include one or more departments or single classes. Children may sit with their families (this is to be preferred) or attend as class or department units. There may be a children's sermon or story, but this is not essential. This flexibility makes it possible to integrate the experience of church attendance very effectively into the church school curriculum.

The plan is peculiarly appropriate to the situation in which the church school meets parallel with the church service. Participation in the church service on Sundays when it occurs is substituted for worship in the church school, but class sessions are held as usual. However, since the time devoted to worship will usually be somewhat longer than that allowed for church school worship it may be desirable in such a situation to limit church attendance to occasional Sundays so as not to encroach unduly on class-teaching time.

3. A distinctive type of family service may be planned. This is distinguished from the usual church service in that it is especially designed for participation throughout by the whole family. Its content seeks to meet the needs of younger members as well as of those who are older. It will

have elements which are appropriate for both, but when a choice has to be made, it will be as often in favor of the youngest members as of those who are more mature.

There are two main ways in which family services may be provided. One way is to adapt the regular service on occasional Sundays so as to take account more fully of the needs and interests of all ages. The other is to have a brief every-Sunday service for the whole family as an integral part of the church school, followed by teaching sessions for all ages.

1. Normal occasions for family services of the first type are such special days as Rally Sunday, Thanksgiving, Christmas, Youth Sunday, Easter, Festival of the Christian Home (Mother's Day), and Church School Sunday (Children's Day). Other Sundays may be chosen, depending on how many such services are desired. In case the church school meets at the some hour with the church service, it will be omitted on such Sundays in favor of church attendance. This is a dramatic way of recognizing that Christian education embraces attendance at church. On the negative side, this does break the continuity in the teaching program, which should not happen too frequently.

Such a family service is not just a regular service with children present. The order of service may be basically the same as on other Sundays, but adaptations need to be made in the choice of hymns, responsive reading, selection of the scripture lesson, and length and content of the pastoral prayer and the sermon, so as to give children a sense of acceptance as part of the congregation and an opportunity for maximum understanding and participation. (It is well to dispense with lengthy anthems.) Whatever the customary length of the service, on family Sunday it should be kept within an hour. If this means omitting an anthem, a second scripture reading, or shortening the sermon, let this be done. The Lord will probably forgive such omissions if they enhance the joy of children in coming into his house.

2. A family service of the second type will usually be the first event of the day, preceding the teaching program. It will be recognized as a service of the church, held in the sanctuary, and conducted by the minister, but it will also be a part of the program of Christian education. Whole families will arrive together and sit as family units. It will be brief—twenty to thirty minutes at most. This is not a Sunday school opening exercise. It is not an adult service with children merely present. It is not a children's service, pitched to the level of the youngest child. It is worship for a whole congregation, with children, youth, and adults all having a considered place in it.

The usual church liturgy may be used, with simplification and adaptation to bring it into the time schedule and within the ability of younger members to participate. Vestments, ceremonials, music should be used. A service of this type is appropriate for the ministry of the junior and youth choirs, but their primary function should be to assist the congregation in corporate worship. The brief time will make it undesirable to have an anthem, except perhaps on special occasions. The chief point of difference from the general service will be the sermon. This must be brief—perhaps five to seven minutes—and whereas in the general service the sermon is chiefly for those who are mature, in the family service it is addressed more to the younger worshipers. This does not mean that it may not also speak helpfully to the religious needs of their parents. The sermon, and in fact the whole service, may at times open questions and issues which will carry over into class discussions.

Following the benediction there will be a teaching program for all, which should continue for fifty minutes or an hour. There will be no additional group worship during the teaching period, though there may be education in worship, and prayer at the opening and closing of class sessions. The full purpose of this plan will not be achieved unless it is accepted as a "package," with all coming for the family service and all remaining for the class period.

The following is suggested as a typical order of worship for a family service:

Prelude
Call to Worship
Invocation
Hymn
Scripture
Sermon
Prayer
Offering and Response
Hymn
Benediction
Postlude

All of this can be done within the suggested time limit. The time required depends not so much on the number of elements as on the time taken for each. Considering the character of the congregation, brevity and dispatch are important in the family service.

Does such a family service meet the worship needs of the parents who would otherwise attend the general church service? The answer should be affirmative, with the possible exception of the sermon. It is to be expected that most adult churchgoers want more than a five-minute sermon with its major content addressed to children. There are two things that may be said to them which will answer their objection in part: (a) the adult class that they attend will give them some equivalent of what they miss in the sermon; (b) they can also attend the general church service which follows the class sessions.

The above discussion on the relation of Christian education to the church service has been rather fully developed because of a strong conviction that the church school cannot operate most effectively without this whole-church experience. This represents a dimension for Christian education for which there has been little specific planning. To make any of the above plans operationally effective requires that the committee on Christian education include the church service in its plan for a total program. In this it will need to work in close cooperation with the minister, the board of deacons, and the church music committee. While individual department leaders and class teachers may arrange a church experience for their pupils, it is better to have an overall plan, which can only be devised by the committee on Christian education in cooperation with others who are responsible for the church service.

WORSHIP IN CHURCH SCHOOL DEPARTMENTS

Whatever plan for participation in the general worship of the church may be worked out, there will also be some provision for worship in the church school. The prevailing custom is to have a worship service in each department, properly graded to the age of the pupils. In smaller churches, because of limited numbers and facilities, there may need to be some combination of departments, but the purpose of graded worship will not be realized if too wide an age span is included. In earlier days it was standard practice to have the whole church school meet together for worship (or "opening exercises," as it was called) but I see little value in this. It is likely to become a substitute for church worship, and any values which it may have can be better achieved by one of the plans for family services discussed above.

If there is no planned provision for participation of church school pupils in the worship of the congregation, the church school must of necessity supply this important part of the Christian education curriculum. However, when Christian education is conceived of as embracing the total church experience, there needs to be some rethinking of the function of worship in the church school. Even under these conditions worship has an essential place in the church school, for such reasons as:

1. Christian education is so concerned with worship that without it, what is done in the church school would lack its central motif.

2. Worship should be a part of everyone's experience in the church on every Lord's day. On Sundays when there are no family services, the church school must provide this for children. The corollary to this is that on Sundays when pupils do attend the church service, this will be their major worship experience, and worship in the church school will be omitted or modified to recognize this fact.

3. The values of participating as families in general congregational worship have been emphasized. There is another set of values in worship in smaller groups with those of approximately the same age and experience. The smaller group makes it possible to relate worship more fully to the experience and comprehension of those involved, with hymns, prayers, stories, scripture, and other materials within their range of comprehension. As a gen-

eral rule, the younger the pupils, the more they need to be grouped with others of their own age.

4. There should be a close relation between worship and the total teaching program. This can be best achieved when both worship and teaching are under the control of church school leaders.

5. Training in the meaning and materials of worship is best given in relation to the actual experience of participation. The church school is better adapted to accomplish this than the church service. Pupils may share in planning and leading worship, and thus gain deeper insights.

6. Through participation in the simpler liturgies of worship in the church school, pupils are prepared for taking their place more fully in the general worship of the church.

How should pupils be grouped for worship? This should usually be determined by the curriculum materials in use. The material may be closely graded by single years or group graded on a two-year or three-year cycle. Worship can be fully integrated into the total program only if the pupils in the worship group all have the same curriculum. Limitations in numbers, suitable rooms, and competent leaders may make it necessary to combine two or more of the departments for worship. In such case the integration with the whole curriculum is less practical. A choice needs then to be made between sacrificing some of the integrative value in favor of having worship by departments or following the class-worship plan to be discussed in the next section.

Responsibility for worship is normally assumed by the principal or superintendent of the department. He will usually plan and lead the worship service, but may share his task with teachers and pupils. He may appoint a worship committee to assist in planning the service and in caring for the "sanctuary." It is not practical to have a worship leader who is not otherwise engaged in the work of the department.

The pastor of the church should be a familiar figure in every church school department. He may at times lead the entire service or take some part in it. This will dramatically emphasize the fact that he is the minister to children as well as adults, and that he regards the church school no less important in his ministry than the church service.

Should worship precede or follow classes? Some prefer to have worship first so that pupils will come to it unfatigued, and may be led to approach class sessions in a devotional spirit. Others prefer to have classes first so that teachers may begin their work as soon as the first pupils arrive, and so that teaching may help to prepare for the worship that follows. There is a trend toward the latter in recent curricula. Both plans have arguments in their favor, and either of them may be used satisfactorily. As a practical necessity, when two departments need to use the same worship room, one must have worship before classes and the other after.

WORSHIP IN THE CHURCH SCHOOL CLASS

An alternative to having worship by departments is to have it in individual classes, as an integral part of the whole class session.

The arguments in favor of this plan run as follows: Integration of worship with teaching may be more fully achieved. Worship may come at any appropriate point in the class period, and may vary in length from week to week to suit the occasion. It usually takes place in the classroom,

64

so there is no loss of time in movement from one room to another. It is under the direction of teachers who are fully aware of the total content of the class session. Pupils may share in planning and conducting the service, and in arranging the room for worship, as a normal part of their class activity. It is informal and by that fact may be more closely related to the experience of the pupils. If the pupils attend a family service in the church, there is less danger of having that experience duplicated in a more informal class service.

On the other side are such questions as: Are all teachers willing and competent to assume responsibility for worship? If they are not competent, will they tend to minimize the place of worship? Is a more formal churchly type of worship with a larger department group more conducive to the experience of worship and better training for worship in the church?

The age of the pupils is a factor in judging the relative merits of having worship in classes or by departments. It is now the prevailing practice in departments below primary to make worship an integral part of the total program. This is best adapted to meeting the needs of younger children and no change should be made in the direction of more formal worship for them.

At what age, then, are children ready for a more formal type of group worship? Should the class type continue through the primary department? Primary-age children are capable of participating in a chapel type of group worship, and seem to find it a satisfying experience. Nevertheless the values inherent in the class type are still prominent at this age. Continuation of this type should be carefully considered, if not preferred.

Pupils of junior age are competent to participate effectively and worshipfully in a formal department service. They appreciate the finesse of a well-conducted order of service. They respond positively to ritual and ceremonial. It is a distinct loss for them to be deprived of this experience. This is not to say that the class type is not also appropriate and valuable for them. Both types might well be provided for them on different Sundays.

Beyond the children's division the matter of church school worship is complicated by two other considerations: To what extent do they regularly participate in the church service? What do they have by way of worship in youth groups? If their worship needs are met in one or both of these, there would seem to be no need for a departmental service in the church school. Otherwise a department service is indicated, with maximum participation on their part in planning and leading. Beyond junior high school all pupils should be so fully involved in the worship of the congregation that a brief devotional period in class is all that is needed in church school.

These additional comments may be helpful in further clarifying the issues and offering guidance to procedure:

1. In general character, the difference between the two —worship by departments or classes—may not be very great. When class enrollment is large, with a group of teachers, the situation is quite similar to that in a department, except that all the workers are involved with all that is done in the group. If the classroom is of ample size and is especially arranged for the period of worship, the setting is not very different from that in which many departments meet. When the department leader cooperates with the teachers and pupils in planning and conducting worship, and relates it closely to the class program, the situation approaches that of worship in a single class.

2. When the pupils regularly attend a family service in the church, or on the occasional Sundays when they do, a more informal period of worship in class is less a duplication of this than a department service. It also presents a better opportunity of preparing for and following up on a family service.

3. It is not necessary to have one or the other type exclusively. Classes that normally have their worship as part of the class session may on some occasions combine with other classes of the department for a joint service.

4. Churches using a closely graded curriculum can completely integrate worship with teaching only when single grades are included in the worship group. Those using departmentally graded materials and having only one class in a given department will find it better to have worship in this single class than to combine with other departments for the sake of having a larger group.

5. It is not very practical for a class to engage in worship unless it has a separate room, except for very subdued prayer, scripture reading, and responses, without music. When two or more classes meet in the same room, as is necessary in some churches, they will usually need to have their worship together.

5 LEADERS OF WORSHIP

Worship is an act of all the people gathered in the presence of God. Its quality and effectiveness depend in large measure on the leader—his preparation for the act and his conducting of the liturgy. He does not worship *for* the congregation. He cannot by any clever device compel them to worship. But more than any other person present he provides the conditions and atmosphere which make it possible for them to enter into worship.

To lead others in the experience of worship is an art that requires the highest qualities of Christian devotion, sensitivity to the mood of others, understanding of the worship experience, and skill in the use of the liturgical forms through which worship becomes a reality. Skill in handling the outer forms of the service needs to be matched with sensitivity to the inner experience of each worshiper without which the outer liturgical forms are empty and meaningless as a noisy gong or a clanging cymbal.

Since worship in the church school is usually conducted by lay men and women there is need for training in this art, even as we expect leaders of classes to be trained in the art of teaching. Failure at this point is obvious in many of our church schools (and even more so in women's groups and other adult programs). Even casual observation will often reveal that there is little understanding of the meaning of worship on the part of both leaders and pupils with consequent lack of skill in leading the service and creating an appropriate setting and atmosphere for it. Our desire for an effective ministry of the laity may well include concern for skill on the part of many to lead others in worship.

In directing the above comments primarily to the need of training for lay men and women, it is assumed that ministers have attained such competence through their professional training and experience. Yet some ministers frankly admit that they are unable to lead younger groups. Unfortunately such admission too often carries with it a lack of concern. Their difficulty is seldom one of not understanding the meaning and significance of worship, but of not being sensitive to the capacities, moods, and vocabulary of children. This is a disability which should not be difficult to overcome if the will to do so is present. Until such skill is achieved there is little chance of having effective family services. Moreover it is important in the Christian education of children that on some occasions they have their minister as worship leader in their separate church school departments.

THE FUNCTION OF LEADERSHIP

What is it that a leader does in worship? He *facilitates* the worship activity and experience of the congregation. Prior to the event of worship he prepares the order of service and provides the setting and atmosphere. As leader of the service he takes the dual role of spokesman for God and leader of the people. As spokesman for God he declares God's word and will in scripture and sermon. What he says and does is not merely his own communication to the congregation, but to the best of his understanding and ability, it is allowing God to speak through him. As leader of the people he seeks to voice their thoughts and aspirations in prayer (which they affirm with "Amen"), directs their expression through ceremonial acts and responses, announces hymns that are appropriate to their sentiments, and calls them to give of themselves and their substance.[1]

This work of the leader will be further clarified by two analogies. Sören Kierkegaard has suggested that a service of worship may be likened to a play. The church is the stage, the members of the congregation are the actors, God is the audience, and the minister and choir are the prompters making suggestions and giving the cues from the wings.[2] In another analogy the congregation at worship may be likened to an athletic game, in which the leader is the coach and the congregation, the team. The coach (worship leader) trains the players and directs the appropriate plays; it is the team (congregation) that does the playing. There is one important exception to both these analogies. The leader is more than prompter in the wings or coach on the sidelines; he is also one of the actors or players by worshiping with the congregation. He might better be identified with the star actor or the captain of the team.

QUALIFICATIONS OF WORSHIP LEADERS

The purpose of this section is twofold: (1) to serve as

---

[1] Cf. Allen O. Miller, *Invitation to Theology* (Philadelphia: United Church Press, 1958), p. 189.

[2] Sören Kierkegaard, *Purity of Heart Is to Will One Thing*, trans. Douglas V. Steere (New York: Harper & Bros., 1938), ch. 12.

guidance for those who are responsible for choosing and appointing workers in the church school; (2) to provide those who have been selected as leaders with a basis for a self-image toward which they may strive in seeking proficiency in leadership.

Spiritual Vitality. To be a sincerely religious person who experiences personally the joy of worship is basic to all else in a worship leader. He cannot communicate what he himself does not possess. Pretense, insincerity, and sham will be readily detected by people of all ages, and especially children. Genuine consecration and devotion, with sincere appreciation of and participation in the liturgy, will be contagious and help to lead others into the mood of worship.

Personal Qualities. It is desirable that the leader have such qualifications as an attractive personality that communicates sincerity and friendliness, the ability to lead others without self-consciousness, a speaking voice that is clear and unaffected, and easy rapport with the pupils he leads.

Understanding of Worship. Effective leadership is based on understanding the nature and meaning of worship, the purpose and nature of the liturgy, the resources that may be drawn on as needed. The foundation for such understanding will be the leader's own worship experience, but he needs to supplement and support this with study so as to achieve both historical perspective and familiarity with current practice in making worship a relevant experience for this generation. He needs to be perceptively aware of the abilities, religious vocabulary, experiences, and needs of the age of pupils whose worship he is to lead. He needs to be familiar with the curriculum of the church school so as to enable him to relate worship to the whole educational experience of the pupils.

Skill in Leadership. Proficiency in the art of leading worship will normally come through experience, but practice must reflect understanding of the leader's function and be guided by self-criticism and thoughtful reflection. Skill in leadership by itself is not enough without being supported by genuine religious devotion, but no amount of piety on the leader's part will make up for a poorly conducted service.

Disciplined Workmanship. The leader who appreciates the sacred office which is his in conducting worship will do his best, before God, to be a workman who does not need to be ashamed (2 Tim. 2:15). He will conscientiously prepare for each service that he is to lead. His preparation will include not only the larger matters of design and content of the service, but will extend to the smaller details which can make or mar it. He will prepare early enough to allow time for mastery of his leadership task and for attention to the details involved in providing the conditions that will best facilitate worship.

Teaching Ability. Leadership of worship in Christian education also involves teaching. Broadly conceived, this includes teaching all the pupils the meaning of worship and an understanding of the liturgy, familiarizing them with new hymns and other content, helping them to engage in appropriate conduct, telling a story and delivering a message effectively. In a more limited sense it includes guiding those who are to assist in the conduct of worship

—teachers and pupils—in the proper performance of their assigned roles.

THE LEADER'S PREPARATION

Timely and adequate preparation is essential. Six steps in preparation may be identified. They are listed and described in the approximate time sequence in which they need to be taken.

Planning the Order of Service. This step should be completed early in the week, and in some cases (as in planning a series of related services) will be begun much earlier than that. The general design may not change greatly from week to week. As indicated in chapter 3, this should include a series of liturgical elements which is fairly constant. Indeed, there is value in having pupils become accustomed to a given order through use of the same for a period of weeks. When major changes are made, these should be explained.

The principal task each week is that of selecting the content for each service. Whatever is included should be tested by the question: Will this help us take a Godward look? Begin by choosing a central theme around which the various elements of the service may be unified. This theme will come to clearest expression in the scripture reading and sermon. Hence these are the first elements of the service to be chosen and planned. The sermon as we are here using the word is the means through which the leader will bring the theme, subject, or problem around which the service is organized to the consciousness of the pupils. This may be done by means of a talk, story, recording, filmstrip, or other effective way. Next, the hymns may be selected which are appropriate to the theme and suitable for the age of participants (see the section on teaching new hymns, pages 91-95) and a prayer selected or composed which is related to the theme in some part of its content. Finally, make your choice of the call to worship, invocation, call and response to offering, benediction, and so on. Since these last items are not usually dependent on the theme, the same words may be used over a period of Sundays.

Building around a theme will tend to give meaning, unity, and freshness to each service, but the effort to do this should not be carried to the extent of destroying the basic character of worship. There should be first a consciousness of coming into God's presence and recognizing his holiness, followed by confession of our sinful nature and acts and the assurance of God's pardon. There should be gratitude for God's goodness and his gracious action in our behalf. Thus far the theme of the service may not be too obvious. The hymn of praise, call to worship, and invocation need not be forced into a given theme, but should be in general harmony with it. The theme will come out most clearly in scripture, sermon, and prayer, and may be reinforced through appropriate hymns. If this general character of worship is violated in favor of emphasis on a theme, there is danger that we will have, not an experience of worship, but another teaching occasion.

The service should be planned carefully so that it will be kept within the appointed time limit. This is accomplished not by omitting essential elements, but by keeping the service simple, conducting it with precision, and holding the scripture reading, prayer, and sermon to desirable brevity.

The completed order of service should be written out, with extra copies for the organist and others who are to participate in leading. For the pupils who are able to read, it is good practice to have copies of the general framework of the service that will be used for a period of time, including the responses in which they are to participate. The leader then needs to supply only the material that is unique to each Sunday—hymns, scripture, sermon, prayer.

Preparing and Gathering Needed Materials. Once the general plan for the service has been decided, the leader needs to take a second step, which is to make sure that all needed resources will be available and ready. If he has selected a story, he must prepare to tell it effectively. If a picture, object, filmstrip or other audio visual is to be used, it must be secured and arrangements made for the use of any equipment that is required. If a drawing or chart is needed, it must be created.

This step in preparation also includes more particular attention to the sermon and prayer. Some form of oral presentation is usually required to articulate and interpret the theme. It is an art to give a short talk which is comprehensible to children and effective with them. Both concept and language must be carefully chosen. Simple words should be used, but they do not necessarily make an abstract concept simple. The presentation should be direct and in conversational style, with no hint of patronizing or talking down. What thoughts are to be communicated and how they are to be expressed, with concrete illustrations, are matters that require forethought and should not be left to the inspiration of the moment.

The prayer is the high moment in worship and should be composed or selected with great care. It is at this point that lay leaders are often most inadequate. They tend to undertake this difficult function without adequate preparation, and consequently make it a medley of pious words and worn religious phrases which can have but little meaning. Read again what was said about the nature and structure of prayer on pages 38-41. While it is suggested that the prayer at some points be related to the theme of the service, this must be done with care lest the leader simply project his thoughts on the pupils, which are in no sense their own. Preparing to lead prayer consists in thinking through in advance what is to be included and how this is to be expressed. If the prayer is not written in full, at least some notes should be made to help in recall. If a prayer is selected which is not the leader's own composition, this will be done because it expresses better than he can in his own words what he would like to say. He must be able to accept and read it as if it were his own.

Personal Readiness. This stage in preparation includes two elements: (1) The service that has now been completely prepared needs to be studied, reviewed, and played over in the imagination (mental rehearsal) until it is thoroughly familiar in every detail. It should be so internalized that there will be no uncertainty or confusion in conducting it, no hesitation or stumbling in reading or speaking. (2) The leader should prepare himself spiritually through prayer and meditation to be a true minister of God in leading the service. His prayer will be that this awesome task of leading others in their worship may be done with such sincerity and conviction of its meetness and rightness that it is no longer he who leads but God—through the Holy Spirit—leading through him.

Preparing the Assistants. Others who are to assist in leadership need to be instructed in their assignments. The organist should have a copy of the order of service indicating hymn selections and other pertinent directions. If teachers or pupils are to take certain parts of the service, they need to know just what they are to do, and in the case of pupils, usually need to be rehearsed. If an outside speaker is to participate he needs to understand his particular function in the service, the approximate amount of time available to him, and the exact hour when he is expected. If the work of ushering, taking the offering, and other such services is rotated among pupils, those responsible on a particular Sunday need to be coached in the proper manner of carrying out these tasks.

Preparing the Room. The room in which worship takes place makes a vital contribution to the atmosphere and mood. Early arrival should be an invariable rule for the leader so that he can make sure everything is in readiness. Some leaders make it a practice to attend to some of these matters on Saturday.

When worship is conducted in a chapel or other place designed for worship only, the setting may be fairly stable, but there are still details in preparation that must be cared for—and these details are important. In case worship is to take place in the classroom, there is the additional matter of rearranging the room for this purpose at the proper time. See pages 117-18 for items to be checked to determine that everything is in readiness.

The task of preparing the room for each service may be assigned to a worship committee of pupils, or rotated among the classes of the department, provided that those responsible are clearly instructed in what they are expected to do.

Preparing the Pupils. To enter into the experience of worship requires an atmosphere of readiness—a reverent and expectant attitude on the part of the worshipers. Adults may enter the sanctuary quietly, pause for a silent prayer, sit in meditation during the prelude, and then be ready to engage in worship. Children by their nature are more boisterous and less inclined to thus discipline themselves. Hence the leader of church school worship will be well advised to allow a brief period for establishing the mood of worship.

The leader's own manner of quiet expectancy will help to set the mood. A few moments of silence will tend to quiet the restlessness which often accompanies entering the sanctuary. A word of reminder to the pupils that they are about to engage in worship will help, if the proper attitude in worship has been previously learned. Explanation, when needed, of the service that is about to follow will enhance participation. At times it may be desirable to highlight the theme with a few words of interpretation. All of this is done *before* the service actually begins. Whatever is done should not be overdone, and should be a positive contribution to the service rather than a negative admonition to be quiet and attentive. Out of decent respect avoid that inelegant "s-h-u-s-h . . ." which is so frequently addressed to children!

CONDUCTING THE SERVICE

If all the necessary steps in preparation have been taken, the leader can approach the opening of the service calmly, prayerfully, and in quiet anticipation of God's blessing. His attitude should exemplify what he expects of his pupils and will project itself to them. As the pupils enter, let him be seated in the chancel. At the moment of opening, let him do what is appropriate to give the necessary orientation and create the mood for the service. Then let him again be seated for the musical prelude, during which the candles (if used) will be lighted. Following this let him stand again to announce the opening hymn or give the call to worship and continue through the remainder of the service, giving only such directions as necessary. With small groups and younger children, it is desirable for the leader to remain seated rather than to stand.

There are certain qualities of platform leadership which should be cultivated. A direct and friendly manner, poise, and dignity are desirable. The leader should not be too conscious of himself and what he is doing, but remember that he as a person is only instrumental in helping others come into God's presence. He should read and speak clearly, distinctly, and with feeling. He should practice economy of words in giving directions and announcing hymns and other elements of the liturgy, and avoid anything in manner and speech that interferes with the even flow of the service. He should have a feeling for proper timing which avoids a sense of hurry, and which does not confuse desirable moments of silence with uncertainty in knowing what to do next. He should guard against anything that is incongruous with the spirit of worship, such as general announcements, requests to sing more lustily, correction of misbehavior.

It is suggested that during the department assembly a clear distinction be made between the worship service—which should be kept free from all things extraneous and be desirably brief—and other activities that may be necessary. The latter include preparation of the pupils for worship, learning new hymns and responses, instruction in the meaning of worship, announcements, projected audio visuals that are more instructional than devotional. The worship service itself begins with the prelude and closes with the benediction and postlude; the other activities in the department assembly come before or after. If candles are used, pupils may be taught that when they are lighted we enter upon worship and when they are extinguished it signifies that worship has been concluded. A different quality of pupil behavior may be tolerated during these instructional periods than that expected in worship, though certainly not disorder at any time.

PUPIL LEADERSHIP

Should pupils have a part in planning and conducting worship? A worship committee for the department or class, or an entire class sharing in planning the service, can be helpful for training in the meaning of worship. Also it helps to give pupils a sense that the worship service is their very own, and it gives the leader feedback on pupil understanding and preferences.

Whether pupils should on occasion conduct the whole service or take such parts in it as reading the scripture, leading prayer, giving a talk or story, raises questions more difficult to answer. On the affirmative side it may be said that this practice has such values as the following: Pupils may be more interested when they or their representatives share in leadership; participation in leadership may be the means to greater appreciation of the meaning of worship; it may bring the service more nearly into the experience of others of their own age; it prepares pupils for future leadership.

There is however another side to this question: (1) The normal flow for the mediation of revelation is not from children to children, but from adults to children. It is significant that the biblical record of God's revelation is addressed primarily to adults. Maturity in understanding and experience is desirable in guiding the experience of worship. (2) The qualities of good leadership seldom are sufficiently developed in children to enable them to conduct worship effectively. What they do is more likely to center attention on themselves than to be instrumental in helping others to look to God. (3) When several persons share in conducting the service, there is likely to be some confusion which interferes with the even flow of the liturgy. (4) Worship conducted by children is almost sure to be of lower quality than when this is done by an experienced adult.

The question of pupils participating as leaders must be answered after balancing values and disadvantages. It is my conclusion that the conduct of worship should be the function of the designated adult leader but he will do well to work with a worship committee in planning, and may occasionally invite pupils to assist in leading. In both cases he will make sure that they are properly instructed and well trained in what they are to do. The age of pupils will be an important factor, since pupil participation becomes more and more feasible with increasing age.

6 EDUCATION FOR WORSHIP

Worship is a response of God's people to God himself. It is he who gives both the impulse and the ability to respond. But the manner in which this impulse will be expressed, like any human achievement, is acquired through education, training, and discipline. The impulse to worship is deep-seated in the very nature of man, but how he understands the object of worship, how he expresses this urge, and whether or not he accepts its disciplined practice as a way of life, are subject to Christian education.

This learning is acquired through a combination of experience, instruction, interpretation, and guided practice. It includes both learning to worship and learning about worship.

WORSHIP EDUCATION IN THE CURRICULUM

The act of worship and education in the art of worship are inherent elements in the curriculum of Christian education. The experience that comes through participation in the services of the church school and the corporate worship of the church is basic to meaningful education. But while much is learned through experience alone, experience accompanied by instruction and interpretation is educationally more effective.

Reality and sincerity will be achieved only when there is belief in the existence of God and the possibility of communion with him. The quality of worship depends on man's conception of the character of God and his relation to man. This does not mean that such beliefs need first to be established before worship can be experienced. This would make it impossible for young children to worship. We proceed on the assumption that God *is* and that he is good. In this we are supported by the Christian family and the congregation. Intellectual exploration of God's being and nature will be dealt with in due course, and such studies will be enhanced by prior experience of God in worship.

Education for worship will include understanding, attitudes, and conduct. For better understanding it will seek to answer such questions as: What is God like? What does it mean to worship? How do we worship? What is the meaning and purpose of the liturgy? What is prayer? What is a hymn? Why do we have an offering? It will seek to foster such attitudes as appreciation of the worship experience; a disposition to engage regularly with reverent expectancy in the worship services of the church school and the church; love of good hymns, music, and other elements of the liturgy. It will provide opportunity for learning hymns, responses, and other materials appropriate for use in worship, which may in some cases include memorization. It will seek to help pupils acquire a vocabulary of religious words and acquaint them with religious symbolism.

It will, through interpretation and practice, help them to learn how to conduct themselves in worship.

The whole Christian education curriculum contributes to education in worship. Study of the Bible, the Christian faith, prayer, and specific units on worship, all help to broaden the pupil's understanding and to assist the pupil in acquiring some of the materials that enhance his participation. These are resources on which the worship leader can draw. I am here concerned, however, with what the leader himself must do in direct relation to worship itself to train the pupils in understanding, attitudes, and participation.

Provision for Training. How is the opportunity to be provided for such training? We are not advocating that worship itself be interspersed with instruction and exhortation. This would destroy its mood and orderly movement. The two functions of worship and training in worship should be kept separate.

In case worship is conducted as an integral part of a class session, the necessary instruction and coaching may be given in the time allotted to teaching, in preparation for an uninterrupted period of worship. When the several classes of a department assemble together for a period of group worship, training might still be given in classes, but will probably be more effective if done by the worship leader as a part of the assembly period. He will divide the available time between training and worship, and keep the two distinct.

Here is one way in which this plan might be worked out: Assuming that the department is in assembly for twenty to twenty-five minutes, let this be divided between five to ten minutes for training and ten to fifteen minutes for worship, the proportionate time given to each varying with the need on any particular Sunday. When the pupils come into the assembly room the leader gives the necessary instructions for the day, teaches a new hymn if one is to be used, makes any necessary general announcements, and when time permits adds something toward the understanding and practice of worship. If worship is held prior to class sessions, and pupils come directly to the assembly room, some of this may be done as presession activity for those who are early. (There is a by-product to having the training period first, in that any tardy pupils will probably have arrived by the time worship begins.) It is made clear that this part of the assembly is not worship. At its conclusion the leader by his attitude and actions signals that worship is about to begin. This is the time for the musical prelude and the lighting of candles. The service itself follows without interruptions. Training might also be scheduled after worship, or some might be given before and some after, but with particular care that the allotted time is not exceeded. If a presentation is to be made to the whole group which is not closely related to worship—such as a visiting speaker or an audio visual—this can usually best be done after worship.

Considering the limited time that most church schools have for their work, the question may properly be asked how this additional activity of training in worship can be included without unduly limiting class time. Of course it will take extra time, but anything as important as this deserves a place in the time schedule. If the church school has one hour, the plan that has been suggested will leave thirty to thirty-five minutes for classes. This is hardly adequate, and effort should be made to lengthen church school to at least seventy or seventy-five minutes. By careful planning, some time that is now wasted can be saved by opening more promptly, moving more expeditiously between assembly and classes, eliminating announcements except those that are absolutely necessary for the whole department, and doing some of the training in presession time. It is not essential to have a period for training every Sunday, and when it is omitted the extra time may be devoted to class sessions. The vacation church school with its longer time span provides a good opportunity for much of the training in worship for which there never seems to be enough time on Sundays.

Religious Language. One of the tasks of Christian education is to help the pupil acquire a vocabulary. Religious communication uses many words that are full of meaning for the initiated but foreign to the ear and tongue of the modern child. Words are symbols that are used to convey meaning, but unless they carry the same thought and feeling for the pupils as for the leader, they do not communicate. Both the word-symbol and the meaning for which it stands need to be learned.

One way of dealing with this problem would be to use only words that are already understood. But our language of faith and devotion has many time-tested words for which there is no simple equivalent. Moreover the pupil should be helped to build a vocabulary which he needs for life in the Christian community. The alternative, then, is to help him acquire a religious vocabulary—words with meaning which in subsequent use will evoke the same response of understanding and feeling.

The need for this is not limited to worship. Class teachers also need to be alert to help pupils acquire the meaning of new words. What is thus learned in classes will be utilized by the worship leader. There are, however, some words peculiar to the worship service which the worship leader must teach. A part of this learning will be accomplished by association through usage in a familiar context. Words are learned in relation to the experience in which they have meaning. But this may not do more than give inadequate or even mistaken understanding, hence the need for direct effort in teaching.

Various methods may be used. Meaning may be attached to a word by defining it in terms that are already familiar (as in our common expression "in other words") and by relating it to experience through recall of past experience or experience that is immediately present, for example, "reverence," "confession," "litany," "benediction." Write the word on a chalkboard or chart so that it may be seen as well as heard, and help the pupils to pronounce it clearly. Define and illustrate with synonyms which are already familiar. If the word itself gives a clue to its meaning (for example, worship: worth-ship), point this out. Use the word in a sentence. If it is the name of an object, show that object or a picture of it. Draw out from the group their own ideas of what a word or phrase may mean to them, and when possible use their ideas in building a more accurate meaning. Give illustrative instances of the meaning of abstract words, such as "fatherhood," "brotherhood," "reverence," "covenant." Here is an illustration of how one leader did this:

In *More Children's Worship in the Church School* Mrs. Jeanette Perkins Brown describes how a church school teacher helped her pupils to understand both the concrete and the abstract meanings of "light." After mentioning the kinds of concrete light they knew, such as bonfires, flashlights, candles, light bulbs, lamps, the children were led to give the more symbolic ideas of light. "It makes you good," said one child. "There are good feelings and bad feelings inside you. The bad feelings are like the darkness and the good are like the light that drives away the darkness, and that's like a candle, that tells you what to do." With older children the teacher referred to the Quakers and their dependence upon the "inner light." When asked what this meant, some children replied: "It's mind and ideas"; "knowledge"; "conscience"; it's God."[1]

In addition to word-symbols there are objects, pictures, and acts which have symbolic meaning. Many of the most profound truths of religion are beyond our power to define in prosaic words but require the language of poetry and symbols. Symbols are concrete sense presentations that point beyond themselves to some ultimate spiritual idea or being. They not only help to enrich and beautify the setting for worship but also stimulate thought and feeling.

To list all the symbols which should become a part of the pupil's religious "vocabulary" as he progresses through the church school would be impractical if not impossible. I can indicate only a few to illustrate: the *cross*, signifying Christianity and God's redemptive love and salvation; *candles*—Jesus Christ, the Light of the World; *three interlocking circles*—the Trinity; *ark* and *ship*—the church; *lamb, good shepherd, fish, vine and branches, crucifix*—aspects of the nature and work of Jesus Christ; *open Bible*—the word of God; the *colors* on the altar, pulpit, and lectern—the various changing seasons of the church year. A few illustrations of symbolic acts are: standing, as a mark of respect; the bowed head, the folded hands, kneeling, signifying humility and contemplation which are appro-

---

[1] Ivah Green, "What's That Word?" *International Journal of Religious Education,* January, 1961, pp. 12-13.

priate to the mood of prayer; the raised hands in benediction; the processional toward the altar, signifying approach to God's presence; and the recessional, indicating return toward a life of service in the world.

Pupils can grasp the idea of symbols at an early age because symbols are so much a part of everyday experience—the handshake, the flag, the gestures in the flag salute, a nod or shake of the head, road signs, traffic lights. The task of the leader is to help the pupil to associate meanings with symbols that will on subsequent occasions evoke intellectual and emotional response. The leader can introduce the pupil to symbols, give a clue as to how they came to be associated with religious reality, and tell what significance they have for Christians. From this point the pupil must build his own deepening meaning through continuing association of them with his own religious experience.

The church library should provide the leader with such resources as the book *Our Christian Symbols* by Friedrich Rest; the A-V Kit "Effective Christian Communication" in which No. 3 (*The Religious Communication*) deals with symbols, or at least the manual which accompanies this kit ("Effective Christian Communication" by Maxwell V. Perrow); for use with pupils, the filmstrip *Christian Symbols*. These may be purchased from denominational bookstores and audio-visual services.

Teaching the Meaning of Worship. Some understanding of what we are about when we worship is basic to all other elements in training. This is not accomplished in a single instructional period but is a growing experience, added to little by little as the class or department progresses through the year and as pupils increase in their ability to understand from year to year. When the leader first undertakes the leading of a group at the beginning of the year he may need to give some basic orientation in what they will be doing in the worship period. Further interpretation can be added as the occasion arises in subsequent weeks. Chapter 2 provides the resource material for this aspect of training, but since it was written for the leader, he will need to make the necessary adaptations and simplifications appropriate for the age of pupils with whom he is working.

This part of training will include guidance in proper attitudes and conduct. Pupils should understand that they are to be active participants and not a passive audience; that they should seek to cultivate a mood of reverent expectancy before God; that they should discipline themselves to turn their thoughts Godward; that there are accepted ways of conduct in worship, such as standing for hymns, bowing for prayer, sharing wholeheartedly in singing, responses, unison prayers, and other parts allowing for their participation.

If the general behavior of the group is detrimental to the mood of worship (as is unfortunately the case in all too many church schools), steps need to be taken to correct this. If it is due to lack of understanding of what is expected, it may be corrected by more adequate instruction. If it is due to lack of inner response, there is not much that can be accomplished by admonition; criticism or scolding will not cure the cause. It may be anticipated, however, that friendly guidance, the leader's own example and that of other adults, a program conducive to reverent response, and a growing appreciation of the experience of worship will in time have a salutary effect. In any case, behavior that negates the very essence of worship should not be tolerated.

Interpreting the Liturgy. The order of worship is the organized form of activities through which the experience of worship may be achieved. Pupils should be clear on what they are to do and why they are doing it. Chapter 3 is the leader's resource for this. He will take his pupils behind the scenes and help them to see the purpose of the design and how each element in the order has a particular meaning and place in the total act of worship. This is a recurring element in training, since changes in the order which may be made from time to time will need to be explained.

Teaching Hymns. The church has an invaluable treasure in its hymns and sacred music. Hymns are a chief means of expressing religious aspiration, devotion, and commitment, and hence are an almost indispensable aid to worship. They reinforce teaching through their use of biblical content and allusions, theological implications, and the challenge to service. Through the combination of words with appropriate music they impregnate meaning with emotion. (The "singing commercial," so annoyingly familiar to every television viewer, is the advertiser's way of cashing in on the power of this combination.) To unlock this treasury of Christian hymns and make it freely available to those who are being introduced to the Christian community is the privilege and opportunity of the leaders of worship.

A hymn consists of both words and music which should be inseparably related in learning, though in the process of teaching each may be given separate attention. Selection of hymns for learning and use will be guided by quality, suitability for the age of pupils, and appropriateness to the purpose or theme. A good hymnal which is designed for use with the age for which the leader is responsible is a valuable guide to quality and suitability.

The test of *good quality* should be applied to both words and music. Is the text good poetry? Does it have a sincere religious message? Is it uplifting and ennobling? Does it turn thought and feeling Godward? Are the words and imagery meaningful for our day? Is the tune good music? Does it express the mood of the words? Is it religious in connotation, free from association with secular usage? Is the hymn as a whole worthy of the effort in learning it, and of such value as to bear repeated use?

The choice of hymns which are *entirely suitable* for children is not always practical, and in some cases the leader will have to accept relative suitability. There are of course songs and hymns that have been written especially for children. We would deprive them of their rightful heritage if we did not let them learn and enjoy these. We would deprive them of an important vehicle through which to express their worship. But as children's hymns are outgrown, they will need gradually to be replaced by some of the great hymns of the church. It is surely an urgent task of Christian education to introduce pupils to this heritage of hymnody. Also, as soon as children are included in common worship, they need to become familiar with the hymns sung in church. Hence some of the hymns most commonly used should also be included in church school worship.

I would suggest as a working principle that some understanding of what they are asked to sing is necessary if pupils are to engage in meaningful worship, but that this does not need to go to the extent of complete understanding of every word and phrase. Many great hymns have depths of meaning which will be fully appreciated only as time and increasing maturity bring new insights. For example, a fairly young child can share in singing the Doxology as an expression of his worship even though the concept of "Father, Son, and Holy Ghost" (the Trinity) is only superficially understood. Let the leader go as far as he can in giving sense to the words of hymns, but leave something for future learning.

The *appropriateness* of a hymn refers to the place it serves in the liturgy and its relation to the theme of the service. Pupils will readily learn that there are hymns of adoration and praise, hymns which are devotional and prayerful, hymns which express commitment and response to human need, and so forth. A repertoire of these various types of hymns should be acquired so as to be available as needed. If a hymn chosen for its relation to a particular theme is already familiar, the leader need only to call attention to the reason for its choice. In many cases, however, its relation to a chosen theme may be the occasion for introducing a new hymn.

Writing particularly for primary-age children, Barbara Kinney Hargis has given the following very helpful "guide-posts for choosing songs":

1. Concrete words containing understandable religious concepts—avoid symbolism.
2. Easy intervals—no wide jumps or tricky halftones in the melody.
3. Simple rhythms.
4. Easy range—about one octave, generally within the staff or not lower than middle C.[2]

The leader should keep a list of the hymns that his

---

[2] Barbara Kinney Hargis, *In the Image of God* (Philadelphia: United Church Press, 1963), p. 35.

pupils have learned as a reservoir on which to draw in future planning. This can be done by keeping a file of the orders of service that have been used in the course of the year, and such a file will also be useful in subsequent years if he continues to lead the same class or department.

The following procedure in teaching a new hymn has been found useful by many leaders. Variations can be made to suit individual preferences.

1. Help the pupils to understand that the singing of a hymn is an exercise of mind as well as of voice. A great teacher of hymnology, Prof. H. Augustine Smith, used to say, "Sing from the nose up as well as from the nose down." Unless there is this dual response—mentally to the thought content of the words, emotionally to the music and poetry —the hymn does not serve its true purpose in worship.

2. Study the words. Through interpretation, discussion, illustration, the use of pictures, and other means, help pupils to understand the meaning of the words and to develop appreciation. Encourage pupils to offer their own suggestions of what the words mean. Their responses often reveal surprising insights, while at the same time they help the leader to gauge the level of their understanding. Have pupils select illustrations from the picture file of what they think the hymn writer is saying. Give whatever interesting information is available about the author and composer, the experience that inspired the hymn, or the occasion for which it was written. In some cases a new dimension of meaning may be added by using a stanza of a hymn as a call to worship, prayer, or benediction.

3. Learn the tune. This may be anticipated and enhanced by having the organist use it as a musical prelude, offertory, or postlude. In the training period, ask the pupils to listen while the tune is being played; let them

hum the tune; sing it for them. Then put the words and music together and let them sing, with additional coaching as needed. Some leaders may not feel competent to lead a group in singing or to demonstrate how a hymn should be sung. If this self-judgment is correct, they may be able to call on a teacher or some other adult to do this, under their direction. If a recording of the hymn is available, it might be used to good effect. The director of music for the church might be asked to help church school departments on certain occasions. The writer found it exceedingly useful to have a teacher of music in a local college come into a junior high department for a number of Sundays to teach them how to sing hymns.

The following suggestions on how to teach a song, by Mrs. Hargis, will be helpful:

1. Know the song thoroughly.
2. Introduce the song when it will heighten the experience of the group.
3. Make the words of the song come alive through the use of charts, posters, pictures.
4. Let the children hear the song in its entirety, words and music.
5. Use only the melody when teaching the song.
6. Avoid drilling the song. It should bring gladness, not groaning, when used.
7. Once learned, use it frequently so that the children live with the song.[3]

Music. Apart from hymns, music serves to enrich worship. Hence there is need for training in music appreciation. Children should have the opportunity to enjoy hear-

---

[3] *Ibid.*

ing the church organ played, and this can usually be arranged with the organist. Recordings may be used with good effect. Leaders of children's choirs should regard education as their main objective.

A good accompanist is an invaluable asset in leading worship and in worship training; also in the teaching of music appreciation. This function should not be assigned to just anybody who can pick out a tune. The best available musicians in the church need to be enlisted, and they should regard their service of equal significance with that of church school teachers. Understanding and cooperation between leader and accompanist are essential.

Prayers. This element in training for worship begins with teaching the nature and meaning of prayer. The pupils should learn that prayer is communication with God—bringing to him "the soul's sincere desire" in word and thought, and waiting in quiet contemplation for his answering revelation.

Here are some suggestions of what the leader may do in making the prayers meaningful for the pupils:

Teach them what is properly included in a prayer—adoration, confession, thanksgiving, supplication, submission, dedication.

Help them to understand that when the leader speaks or reads a prayer he is trying to express the aspirations and petitions of all present, and that they should follow his every thought as if it were their own.

Let them join (regularly or occasionally) in the "Amen" as an affirmation that they have accepted in spirit the prayer that has been offered.

When pupils join in unison prayer, help them to do so with understanding and feeling.

At times let them help make the prayer by suggesting what they would like to have the leader include.

Encourage an individual or a group to compose an original prayer for inclusion in the service.

Teach them that moments of silent prayer are not occasions for "wanderings of mind" but for each to make his own prayer.

Help them learn the language of prayer through study of classic prayers, including the Lord's Prayer—which is so frequently used but often without understanding or self-involvement in the words that are so glibly recited.

Let your own prayers be well planned and expressed in language which is beautiful and dignified but also simple and direct, so that they may be living examples of what you are trying to teach.

If a pupil is to lead prayer, let someone help him to do this well so that it may also be the occasion for him to learn more about the meaning of prayer.

The Offering. An offering is included in the service of worship, not because it is a convenient way of collecting money, but because the giving of substance is an act of worship. What we are and have is a gift from God and in our offering we render to him a portion of what he has given us. In early days people in their worship brought offerings from the best of their harvest—fruits of their fields and flocks. In our day money has come to represent our possessions.

Pupils may have only vague notions of why they bring an offering. Education in the meaning of the offering will have two aspects: (1) why we have an offering in worship, and (2) what the objectives of our gifts are. We give because we love God and seek in every way to do his will.

Through our gifts we respond to our faith that the world and all therein, including ourselves, belong to God; we give in thanksgiving for what God has done for us. Our gifts are a symbol of the giving of ourselves. There are appropriate scripture verses and songs that express the meaning of Christian giving, which may be spoken or sung at the time of the offering, such as "All things come of thee, O Lord; and of thine own have we given thee"; "We give thee but thine own, whate'er the gift may be; all that we have is thine alone, a trust, O Lord, from thee"; and the Doxology.

The causes that will be supported by the offering should be understood, appreciated, and appropriated. This is closely related to education in the work and mission of the church as she seeks to do God's will among men. Gifts are made so that the church can exist and serve; they are needed for maintenance, local program, good works, and missions.

Normally offerings will be made to the work of the church, and this is a part of educating pupils to identify themselves with their church. Special giving projects, chosen by the pupils themselves, are helpful in relating them more directly to the purpose of their giving, but should not be a substitute for giving to and through the church budget. With younger children in particular, the large categories in the church budget may need to be interpreted with specific instances of what they include. For example, in a church that was engaged in a building project, two departments of the church school were invited to accept as their task the giving of the money to provide for a cross on the steeple, which they did with enthusiasm. Giving for world ministries can be dramatized by stories and pictures of individual children and their families to whom the mission of the church is being extended or of the work of particular missionaries. Although we are dealing here in particular with offerings of money, the broader aspects of stewardship as self-giving in Christian life and work should not be neglected.

Education for the Sanctuary. Throughout our consideration of worship in Christian education we have assumed that it will have some relation to the common worship of the church, as a present experience and as preparation for lifelong participation in public worship. Important as is class or department worship, it is in the church service that the full significance of God's people at worship will be met. Here we have the full liturgy of which the department or class service is an adaptation. Here we have a room designed for worship only, with beauty and richness of symbolism, which provides a setting that can only be approximated in church school rooms. Here the pupil may experience the exaltation that comes with being a part of a whole congregation at worship.

These values will not be realized unless there is education and interpretation related to worship in the sanctuary. Pupils may on occasion be taken to the sanctuary when it is not in use so that they can experience its beauty and be instructed in its design and furnishings. They should be helped to identify the symbols and their meaning, study the stained-glass windows, and learn the names and functions of parts of the room and the appointments—narthex, nave, chancel, aisle, choir, pulpit, lectern, altar, font or baptistry, dossal. The pastor is the ideal person to give this instruction. On occasions when children are to attend church, the printed calendar should be available in advance so that the order of service may be reviewed and interpreted. If hymns to be used are unfamiliar, they may be reviewed before the service. Some introduction to the sacraments can be given by having children attend and observe on Sundays when there are to be baptisms or the celebration of the Lord's Supper.

TRAINING LEADERS OF WORSHIP

Training workers for leadership of worship is at least as important as training for teaching. All the workers in the church school should have an understanding and appreciation of the worship aspect of the curriculum, so as to enable them to share in and support by their teaching what the leaders are doing. For those who are to lead in worship this training needs to be more intense and in greater depth.

Most persons who are called to such leadership have had no previous training and experience, other than as pupils in the church school, members of the congregation, and perhaps as teachers having observed others lead worship. The important thing for them is not the point where they begin but how quickly they proceed toward acquiring understanding and proficiency. Much of this training will need to be acquired through efforts at self-improvement— learning on the job through practice and study.

There are a number of resources to which leaders may go for guidance and training. The coursebooks in the church school curriculum are perhaps the most important. These usually provide general considerations on worship and also specific suggestions in relation to the work to be covered on each particular Sunday. Books on worship offer a rich resource for more intensive study. These should include some which deal with Christian worship in general and some with worship in the church school more specifically. (See chapter 11 for suggestions.) Institutes and training schools may offer courses on worship, or courses on departmental method including worship, for which leaders may enroll. Consultations with the pastor, superintendent, and other experienced workers may help the new leader to get off to the right start and to profit from continuing guidance.

Those responsible for the training and supervision of workers in the church school should give particular attention to the needs of leaders of worship. In this the minister can be very helpful because of his own training and his concern for developing a worshiping congregation. Here are a few suggestions: (1) devote an occasional general workers' conference to a consideration of worship; (2) have specialized conferences for all those who are engaged in worship leadership; (3) have consultations with individual leaders, especially when they are first getting started; (4) provide library resources for the use of worship leaders; (5) help leaders to have the best possible setting for worship through providing good equipment, assignment of available rooms, and adjustment of time schedules; (6) visit departments and classes and discuss the program with leaders on the basis of observation.

The following questions should be helpful to worship leaders in evaluating themselves and their work. They may also serve as a basis for evaluation by a visiting supervisor and for subsequent discussion between the leader and the visitor.

1. Was the service well prepared in advance, with proper spiritual preparation of leaders and pupils prior to the service?

2. Does the service have good design, centering in a

theme, and are the materials used so related to the theme as to provide unity?

3. Does the service center on the worship of God (not the entertainment of the pupils) and have something important to say about his relation to us and our relation to him?

4. Do the materials used give a Christian interpretation of God and are they within the comprehension of the pupils? (Note especially the prayers of the leader.)

5. Do the hymns have literary and artistic merit, and are they suited to Christian worship?

6. Is the leader sincere and reverent, and does his attitude inspire the spirit of worship?

7. Is there reverent good order, with pupils attentive and responsive, participating in singing and responses, and seeming to achieve communion with God?

8. Are the ushering, offering, and other elements in which pupils share handled effectively and with reverence?

9. Is the room well arranged, clean, orderly, properly heated and ventilated?

10. Is opportunity provided in the session for training in worship? (This may not be necessary in every session but the results of training should be evident.)

7 ROOMS FOR WORSHIP

God is not confined to a particular place. Worship—the meeting of God with man—may happen anywhere at any time. Jesus said to the woman of Samaria, "The hour is coming when neither on this mountain nor in Jerusalem will you worship the Father. . . . God is spirit, and those who worship him must worship in spirit and truth" (John 4:21, 24). What is important is the reality of the divine-human encounter, not the place where it happens. These considerations should keep us from identifying worship with a particular place, or confining it to a time when people are gathered in such a place.

Nevertheless, from a practical standpoint, group worship does require a place and a setting in which God's people gather for the purpose of meeting God. This may be a home, an outdoor retreat, any room in the church building, or the church sanctuary. Such meeting places for worship have always had an important role in religion, by whatever name they have been called—sacred place, temple, shrine, church, cathedral, chapel. They serve not only as a meeting place for the people, but also as a place where God's presence is experienced in a peculiar way. In considering worship in the church school, it is necessary that we give some thought to the setting in which the services are conducted.

There are two conditions which should characterize a room as an appropriate setting for worship: worthiness and practicalness.

1. It should respect and honor God's holiness through beauty, quiet dignity, cleanliness, and symbolic expression of theological convictions concerning God's relation to his people.

2. It should facilitate the mood and practice of worship through its size and dimensions, arrangements, furnishings, symbolism, and emotional association. This does not suggest that worship can be induced by psychological manipulation through symbols, aesthetic appeals, or other gadgets. Nevertheless people are subject and sensitive to atmosphere and suggestion, which may be either helpful or hindering. What we are seeking is a setting that will assist in turning the mind and soul Godward. This is more likely to happen in a well-ordered, reverence-inspiring, and aesthetically satisfying church or chapel than in a room which is haphazardly improvised and poorly appointed and arranged.

THE PLACE FOR WORSHIP

The following discussion of the appropriate characteristics and requirements of a building or room which is to serve as a place for public worship is introduced for two purposes: (1) to help leaders in the church school understand better and appreciate more, and in turn interpret to their pupils, what the church has provided for the worship activity of the congregation; (2) to serve as a guide in making the best use of other rooms, which need to be arranged for use as worship chapels for departments and classes, but in the course of the day or week may need to serve other needs as well.

What have Christians done in building and equipping a room that is to serve as a setting for worship? With many variations in detail due to historical development, contemporary needs and styles, and local preference, churches generally will have the following:

Nave. This is the area for the seating of the congregation. It is usually oblong, twice or three times as long as it is broad, with center aisle and side aisles. Windows may be of clear glass, through which the outside world can be seen as a reminder that while the congregation at the moment is gathered for worship, its mission and service is in the world outside. Or windows may be of richly stained glass, depicting symbols or scenes of biblical or historical events or characters, as visual reminders of the church's faith, history, and the continuity of the present with the past. The nave is usually equipped with pews for comfortable seating, and in some denominations with kneeling benches in front of the pews. Racks for hymnbooks and other needed materials are fastened to the backs of pews. A baptismal font (in churches practicing infant baptism) is usually placed on the main floor near the chancel, or just within the chancel.

Chancel. This is at the front end (sometimes designated as "east") of the nave, and symbolizes God's peculiar presence and holiness. If a cross is used, it is placed at the focus of attention in the chancel—suspended over the altar, fastened to the front wall, or placed on the altar-table. The altar-table (I am using this compound word because in most Protestant churches there is no clear distinction between altar and communion table, and both symbolize the presence of God) occupies the center of the chancel, either against the front wall or standing free. Back of the altar-table there may be an ornamental screen called reredos, or a curtain or drapery called dossal or dorsal.

Within the chancel there is provision for the seating of the ministers, and a pulpit and lectern for the performance of the ministerial functions. Usually the pulpit is at one side of the chancel and the lectern at the other, although in some cases a single piece of equipment at front-center serves both purposes. On the lectern is usually found an open Bible. The ministry of music may also be located in the chancel with places for the choir and the organ console.

Other items that may be found in the chancel are a table for offering plates and stands for flowers. In the case of churches that practice baptism by immersion, a baptistry is provided in relation to the chancel and in clear view of the congregation. In churches that have communicants come forward for the Lord's Supper, there will be a communion rail and kneeling bench at the forward edge of the chancel.

Narthex. This is a vestibule or room at the entrance to the nave, at the opposite end from the chancel (sometimes designated as "west"), separated from the nave with sound-resistant walls and doors. This should be spacious enough to serve as a waiting room for those who come late and will be admitted to the service at appropriate times, and as a place where people may greet the minister and one another after the service. People should learn that when they pass through the doors into the nave, the time for silence and quiet meditation has come. All conversation should be confined to the narthex.

These, in brief, are the traditional arrangements and furnishings which may be found in some form in almost any church. They symbolize a theology of worship that sees God's people gathered for his worship, facing toward a chancel with its altar and other symbols signifying God's presence in a peculiar way. This theology recognizes a ministry set apart from the people and speaking for them to God, and to them as messenger of God's word, seeking to lead them into an experience of God's presence.

In recent times there has been some experimentation with arrangements which symbolize a different doctrine of the church, namely, that God is in the midst of his people and that all are ministers as well as seekers of his grace. This has led to elimination of the chancel and placement of the altar-table and pulpit in the midst of the congregation, with seating arranged around them. Such experimentation recognizes desirable flexibility in providing a room and arrangements which best express contemporary thought concerning the meaning and practice of public worship.

WORSHIP CHAPELS

In addition to the chief room for the worship activity of the whole congregation, some churches provide smaller, more intimate and informal chapels. A chapel may be used for smaller groups on various occasions, such as lenten services, prayer meetings, weddings, youth groups, and departments of the church school. The arrangements, furnishings, and symbolism should be the same as those described above, although usually more simple.

If the chapel is to be used for both adults and children, a

practical compromise needs to be found with respect to the height of pews, lectern, and pulpit. There should, however, be no compromise on its adequacy to serve the purpose of public worship, with the same attention given to dignity, beauty, symbolism, and functional utility as in the church sanctuary. One may also find chapels designed particularly for children, in which case the adaptations need to be more radical to suit the needs of a younger congregation. With the recent emphasis on family worship in the church and on the integration of worship into class sessions, there has been less concern with providing a chapel distinctly for children.

CHURCH SCHOOL ROOMS FOR WORSHIP

As emphasized in previous chapters, the worship aspect of the curriculum includes worship with the whole congregation, worship in departments or combinations of departments, and worship in church school classes. When the setting is the church sanctuary or a chapel, the concern of the Christian educator with respect to the worship room is only one of interpreting and properly using what has already been provided. When the setting is some other room—which is usually the case for departments and classes—much thought needs to be given to equipment and arrangement so as to provide an environment conducive to worship.

Sanctuary and Chapel. In view of the fact that sanctuaries and chapels have been especially designed for worship they are the most appropriate for this purpose. Persons of all ages should have the experience of worshiping in this setting. Such experience needs to be enriched through education in the meaning of the sanctuary. This can best be given at times when a department or class visits the sanctuary to see that which is being interpreted. In this the assistance of the minister and organist can be very helpful.

By the time he reaches the age of ten or eleven a pupil should recognize, be able to identify by name, and understand the purpose of the three parts of the sanctuary—narthex, nave, and chancel—as well as of the major furnishings. He should have some understanding of the theological and symbolic significance of the architectural form and arrangements. He should be familiar with the chief symbols in his own church; and if there are stained-glass windows, he should know what they depict. Such education in the meaning of what the church provides for its congregation will help in his understanding of worship and tend to enrich his experience when he joins the congregation in this place. It will help also in his appreciation of whatever provisions are made for worship in his own department or class, and enable him to share in making these rooms as appropriate as possible.

Department Rooms. Most church schools have worship by department groups, either regularly or occasionally. It would seem logical for these departments to use the one place that has been built and equipped for the sole purpose of worship—the church sanctuary. This is not usually done for reasons of nonavailability when needed and unsuitability because of size and formality of arrangement. Young children in particular may respond better in a room adapted to their needs in size, equipment, and atmosphere. If the sanctuary is to be used by the church school, priority should be given to older departments.

When the sanctuary is used for a church school department, either by choice or from necessity, some leaders attempt to meet the problem of oversize by having the group meet in the pews at one side and not using the chancel. This is not good practice. The architectural and aesthetic impact which gives the sanctuary its appropriate atmosphere is largely negated when the chancel is bypassed. It is better to concentrate the group in the front-center of the nave and conduct the service from the chancel.

If a chapel is available it may serve as a place for worship for a number of departments on a rotation plan. At any church school hour it may be used by two departments—one having worship at the beginning of the hour and the other at the end. Extension of use to more than two departments is possible through a plan whereby no department meets as a whole group every Sunday, but alternates this with worship in class.

The more usual situation is one in which department leaders need to adapt a room for worship that has not been specifically designed for this purpose—which in fact may in some cases be very inappropriate, such as a large fellowship hall, a dining room, or a gymnasium. However, ingenuity and imagination can convert almost any room into a "sanctuary" that embodies some of the elements of the beauty of holiness and meets the conditions which facilitate worship. Because of the importance of the environment in providing a favorable atmosphere, no effort should be spared in providing a place that is an honor to God and a suitable meeting place between God and man. To this end the following suggestions are offered.

1. Consider the room as a whole and decide what arrangement will be best, bearing in mind the general characteristics of a good setting for worship. Insofar as the properties of the room allow, try to achieve the following: For the chancel choose that end of the room which is

opposite the entrance, and if the room is oblong, that end which has the shorter wall so as to allow for a setting in depth. This should preferably be a blank wall without windows, to avoid facing pupils toward the light. If windows cannot be avoided they may be treated with draperies to reduce glare to a minimum.

In general strive for an atmosphere of sanctuary, a place for withdrawal from the world for communion with God, leading in turn to renewal of perspective and strength for the daily task. Do all you can to make it a place of quiet beauty through attractive arrangement, appropriate wall and ceiling colors, window curtains, perhaps a few suitable framed pictures attractively hung, and scrupulous cleanness and order. Carpeted aisles and chancel floor will aid materially in accomplishing this. If at times projected pictures are to be used, opaque shades or draperies may be permanently installed to be readily available when needed but unobtrusive when not in use.

2. Arrange the front of the room as a chancel. This will be planned in general after the pattern of the church chancel, though usually greatly modified and simplified. It is desirable to have the floor of this area raised a few inches above the level of the nave, but this is not essential, and not necessary if the groups using this room are small. If the room is used primarily for worship the chancel furnishings may be permanently installed; if also used for various other purposes they should be movable and properly placed for each worship occasion.

The equipment and arrangement of the chancel may be as follows:

What corresponds to an altar-table will occupy the focus of attention. This should be an object of beauty and religious suggestion. Since this is not an altar or a communion table, let us call it simply a "worship center." It should consist of an oblong table placed against the front wall and backed appropriately with a dossal curtain. The table may be covered with an attractive cloth. It will be simply furnished. What is placed on it will vary with the age of the pupils, and may be changed from time to time in harmony with the seasons and the theme of the services. It should be a means to help create the mood and atmosphere of worship.

> We cannot see God, but we can resort to symbols suggestive of his presence and of the significance of our own act of worship in his presence. Each picture, each object having for us some religious association and meaning, helps us to focus our spiritual attention upon the Divine Reality.[1]

Candles in matching candlesticks may be placed at each end of the table. (The use of candles by early Christians was probably utilitarian, for the simple purpose of giving light, but for us they have come to have symbolic meaning, such as the light of the gospel or Jesus the Light of the world.) At the center of the table there may be an open Bible, a cross, a flower arrangement, a globe, a picture, or some other object or symbol which has significance. This is enough. To add more could be distracting rather than helpful.

> With . . . young children . . . there may be an interest table or beauty spot around which little groups gather informally with a leader, entering into moments of spontaneous joy and wonder which are really worship. . . . A low table with flowers or other nature objects, a simple arrangement of figurines, or a picture is all that is necessary. It is impor-

---

[1] Irwin G. Paulsen, *The Church School and Worship,* ed. C. A. Bowen (rev. ed.; Nashville: Abingdon Press, 1940), p. 66.

tant that the table be low enough to come within the eye-range of a small child, that the arrangement be simple enough not to confuse him, and that it be within the scope of his appreciation and understanding.[2]

At one side and toward the front of the chancel there should be a pulpit and on the other side a lectern (not needed, however, in the case of young children's groups). These should be attractive and of proper height for the pupils who are to share in leadership. It is not conducive to effective leadership to have the lectern so high that the leader's head can scarcely be seen above it. Adjustable height is desirable in case pupils of different ages are to be accommodated. The same purpose may be achieved through having a box or substantial stool on which smaller pupils will stand when they lead. If practical considerations do not allow for the use of both a pulpit and lectern, one may serve the purpose of both, but it should still be placed at one side to avoid obstructing a clear view of the worship center.

In the chancel there will also need to be seats for those who are to participate in leading the service, and for a choir if necessary. These seats can best be placed against the side walls, facing toward the center and not toward the congregation. Small tables or stands may be placed at either end of the worship center for offering plates and flowers. It is not good practice to place offering plates on the worship center.

If projected pictures are to be used on occasion in the worship service, or before or after the service itself, a screen may be worked into the wall treatment back of the

[2] Alice Louise Brown, "Worship Centers for Children," *International Journal of Religious Education*, September, 1948, p. 4.

worship center. It will normally be hidden from view but can easily be drawn into place for use when needed. Another plan is to have a screen inconspicuously mounted on the wall at one side. This will avoid the distraction that results from having to set up a portable screen in the chancel.

A suitable place will need to be found for a piano or organ, which may be either in the chancel or the nave. If possible, it should be so placed as to make necessary communication (usually by simple signals) between the leader and accompanist unobtrusive.

3. The remainder of the room will be arranged as a nave, which is the seating area for the congregation. Pews or chairs need to be of proper height for the pupils. In case groups of different ages are to use the room, a reasonable compromise in seat height needs to be made. Chairs should be arranged in straight rows facing the chancel, with a center aisle, and side aisles if space permits. If comparatively small groups are to be accommodated, a more informal arrangement may be appropriate, such as a semicircle facing the worship center.

If the room is too large, that portion should be selected for a worship setting which best lends itself to carrying out the design suggested above. If it is the church sanctuary, pupils should be grouped at front-center and the service conducted from the chancel. If it is a fellowship hall (assuming movable equipment) or a dining room, the chancel should be so located as to have a good wall background and the chairs for the congregation grouped as suggested above. The sense of lostness in a big room, can be overcome in a measure by placing screens at either side and back of the area which has been chosen for the worship setting.

If class-teaching, as well as department worship, needs to

be conducted in the same room, each should have its own distinct setting. It is not conducive to good atmosphere and participation to have pupils scattered about the room in class groups during worship. Even if the same chairs need to be used for both purposes, these can be quietly carried by the pupils from one location to the other, although some training and practice may be needed to accomplish this. With younger children the following procedure is effective in avoiding chair-dragging noises: have each pupil turn around and face his chair, pick it up by the seat, and carry it and quietly set it down in the desired location.

It is exceedingly helpful in keeping rooms in order to have a cabinet or closet for the storage of hymnals, Bibles, audio-visual equipment, worship center furnishings, and other materials when not in use. This may be within the worship room itself, or conveniently adjacent to it.

4. Entrance to the church school worship room will usually be from a corridor without benefit of an area which corresponds to the church narthex. Since pupils will usually enter and leave the nave as class groups, moving directly from and to classrooms, there is no great need for a narthex. If, however, pupils come directly to worship on arrival, it is desirable to have some space outside the door where those who come late may wait until a proper point in the service for them to be admitted. In any case, pupils should learn that there is a definite point at which they pass from outside into the sanctuary and to maintain a respectful decorum while they are within.

5. In these suggestions for rooms for worship it has been my purpose to find ways to provide a setting that corresponds in a measure to that which prevails in the church sanctuary. I feel that this is sound for general guidance.

However, church school leaders are faced with rooms of many different types which they must utilize as best they can. The setting is after all only a means to the end of facilitating genuine worship. All kinds of adaptations of the most ideal arrangement may need to be made to meet the practical necessity. The setting in a given room can only be the best under the conditions provided by that particular room. Leaders who are clear on the general requirements for the best setting should proceed with freedom and ingenuity to make the best possible use of the rooms available to them.

It should also be remembered that at times there may be a radical departure from the traditional pattern with no loss, and perhaps considerable gain, in effectiveness. Such departures may most easily be made with groups other than church school departments which meet for worship at other than the church school hour. Robert Seneca Smith gives the following illustrations:

> Sometimes the service of worship is indoors about a fireplace. A small group is sitting in a semicircle. The lights are dim. The atmosphere invites repose and meditation. The fire, burning low, is the focus of attention. All eyes turn toward it. It is symbolic of warmth, light, cheer, fellowship. Fire has always been associated with worship from most primitive times. In the mood which such an environment inspires, one's thoughts respond naturally and with reverence to quiet music and singing, the reading of poetry, the telling of a story, and simple, earnest prayers. . . .

> There is the familiar out-of-door type of worship, beside a lake or the sea, or amid the mountains. . . . The group is seated on the sloping ground so that no one's view of the lake is obstructed. The leader stands to one side, so that he too may often turn to the lake and the changing colors on the water, the sky, and the hills. Nature has provided her

own focus of attention. Nothing that man may build can compete with such a setting. . . .

Pine trees are like the pillars of a great cathedral, and their branches arching overhead are like its vaulting. One gets seclusion in such surroundings and the wind in the branches suggests the mystery of the coming of God's spirit. . . . The incense is the fragrance of the pines; the music is the sighing of the wind in the trees. Nothing is man-made. Everything is God-made. Nature is symbolizing her Creator.[3]

6. After the best possible setting has been provided, there is further need for constant care to keep it in prime condition. Neglect of this keeps many rooms from being fit places for God's worship. Order, cleanliness, and good taste are essential. A good sexton is a great help, but the leader should be sensitive to the details of reverent care that the room for worship deserves.

Prior to worship the leader should check on such questions as: Is all needed equipment in its proper place? Are the candles on the worship center of equal height? Are the candle holders clean, with spilled wax removed? Are pictures hanging straight, curtains and draperies attractively arranged? Has the room been cleaned and dusted? Are the piano top and other vulnerable places free of accumulated clutter? Have materials and equipment which are not to be used been stored away out of sight? Are chairs spaced neatly in rows? Have hymnbooks and orders of service been distributed, or provision made for their distribution at the proper time? Is the room comfortable—adequately lighted, heated, and ventilated? Are pupils clear on where they are to sit in the nave, or in the chancel in the case of participat-

---

[3] Robert Seneca Smith, *The Art of Group Worship* (Nashville: Abingdon Press, 1938), pp. 66-67.

ing leaders? If projection equipment is to be used, is it ready, or at least available for quick readiness when needed?

It is good practice for worship leaders to visit the church on Saturday for a thorough checkup while there is yet time to correct conditions that need to be remedied. If this is not feasible, then early arrival on Sunday is a necessity. Groups of pupils may serve in rotation as a worship committee or altar guild and perform many of the duties in proper care of the sanctuary. Under the guidance of the worship leader or a teacher they will not only render a useful service but also add to their education in church responsibility and in the meaning and appreciation of worship.

Classrooms. There remains for consideration the setting for worship when it is conducted with a single class as an integral part of the class program. This is generally the pattern for younger children. Hence much of what has been said about worship by departments applies primarily to grade school pupils and older ones. However, there is an increasing tendency to extend the class-type worship into the grades, and even throughout the church school.

If individual classes are taken to a chapel for their worship period, what has already been said about the worship setting is sufficient, except that when limited to a single class the pupils may have a larger role in arranging the room for a particular service, and in the service itself.

The plan of worship by classes usually assumes that it will be conducted within the regular classroom. This of necessity requires that the setting be more flexible and informal. For young children there may be very little formal arrangement—just a gathering of the group for a few minutes around the teacher or the worship center. For older children, if the room is large enough to permit, a portion may be set apart as a permanent worship area.

In simplified form, the suggestions made for the department worship room will apply. More likely the same space will need to be used for other class activities as well as for worship. Chairs will be appropriately grouped for worship at the appropriate time. A simple worship center can be provided, either as a permanent feature or set up each time when needed. A piano, autoharp, or other instrument will be needed unless one of the teachers can lead singing without instrumental aid. Pupils may help to decide how to make their room "churchly" in effect and experiment with different ways of accomplishing this. Let us not be concerned, however, with too much formality, for one of the objectives of class-type worship is informality of setting and easy relevance to the whole class program.

8 WORSHIP IN NURSERY AND KINDERGARTEN

The general nature of worship is the same for all ages. All respond to the same God whose nature and grace do not vary with the age of the worshiper. All are impelled to worship because of basic needs and responses which are common to their human nature: awe and wonder, gratitude, fear of the unknown, a sense of personal inadequacy and unworthiness, a need for ultimate interpretation of existence in terms of a reality and power that is beyond their own.

But the particular ways in which these impulses to worship come to expression do vary with the age of the worshiper. This is necessarily so because worship comes out of experience, and for younger persons is limited by vocabulary and ability to engage in conceptual thinking and to appropriate meaning through symbols. Much of what has been said in previous chapters is basic to understanding how to conduct worship for any age-group. The purpose of this chapter is to offer more specific suggestions on the form and content of worship which is appropriate for preschool children. I acknowledge indebtedness for the contributions to my understanding which have been made by many workers with young children, a few of whom will be recognized by name through quotations from their writings.

There may be some who contend that worship is an experience of maturity and question whether in fact a little child can experience it. No one who has had the privilege of leading children and observing their attitudes and responses is likely to have such doubts. The attitudes that lead to worship are inherent in children—perhaps even more acutely than in those who are more mature. Let us only remember that a child worships as a child, and not expect him to use the words and thought forms of adults. True, there should be a deepening and widening of the capacity for and the experiencing of worship with growing maturity, but this is more likely to occur if the foundations are laid in simpler and yet genuine experiences at earlier stages.

It is desirable that even young children have some acquaintance with the corporate worship of the church, but their participation will be limited. (This limitation applies even to family services, although these present somewhat better opportunity for participation than the corporate worship of the church.) Most of their worship experience will be in their own church school groups. Children should learn to know their minister as a friend and as the spiritual leader of the congregation. This will be accomplished in part through the children's participation at times in the church service, but the minister should also be a welcome visitor and participant in department activities. Leaders who are alert to the desirability of this contact with the minister may well take the initiative in arranging such visits.

In planning the worship activity, department leaders should have in mind such questions as the following: Who are these boys and girls? What is their real life in terms of activities, interests, joys and sorrows, perplexities, temptations, longings, ambitions, and so on? How can we help them understand themselves and their lives in the religious dimension of God's creation, love, and care? What can we do to help them identify with something other than themselves and to express their inarticulate feeling-thoughts in words and actions that have meaning? What materials can we use which are most appropriate to achieve this? How can we relate the moments of worship to other aspects of the day's session so as to make the whole more meaningful?

In current church-school practice children who are two and a half and three years of age are classified as nursery; those who are four and five, as kindergarten. There is a vast difference in maturity between children who are two and a half or three, and five years old—the more so if the five-year-olds are attending day school kindergarten. It is not suggested that they be treated as a single group unless limitations in numbers or space make this absolutely necessary. However, the general character of the program during these years is sufficiently similar to enable us to consider their worship activity in a single chapter.

It is not intended that what follows should be a complete guide to methods and materials of worship in a given department. The purpose is only to give general understanding and direction, in the perspective of the whole theme of worship in the church school. In the more recent curricula the department manuals, teachers' guides, and coursebooks provide general guidance, suggested materials, and other helps for the leader of worship. These are indispensable. The sections that follow seek faithfully to interpret the thought of the writers of these materials, who are specialists in their respective departments.

THE PUPILS

The world of the preschool child, the here and now, is centered in his home. His entrance into the nursery may be his first experience of the world away from home in an environment where his parents are not present, and in which he is surrounded by other children and adults. He is a bundle of dynamic energy which must express itself in action rather than passive confinement to a teaching group. His curiosity is insatiable, his interest span short, his vocabulary limited though rapidly growing, his thinking in terms of things and actions rather than abstract concepts. He craves acceptance and affection, and will often express his feelings bluntly in words and actions. He operates largely in terms of his own interests. His ability to cooperate with others and to participate in group activity develops only gradually. What he now is has been—and continues to be—greatly influenced by his home background.

The child who is accustomed to prayer in the home, a natural inclusion of religion in conversation, and pictures and stories that have religious implications, and whose parents are actively interested in the church, is more ready to engage in worship in the church school than his fellow pupil who has not had such experience. All of this points to the need for teachers to know and accept children as they are, to plan a program which capitalizes on this understanding, and to work as closely as possible with the parents.

THE PROGRAM

While it is my purpose to deal primarily with worship, this is so intermingled with the rest of the program that I must first take a look at the session as a whole. One of the hardest lessons for new teachers of young children to learn is that the most desirable program allows for a great deal of free activity. These children are not yet ready to sit around a table during a large part of the class period for content instruction under the direction of the teacher. In fact, the amount of time they can spend profitably in meeting as a formal group is very limited. In the nursery there should be no compulsion on any child to join in group activity if he feels disinclined to do so.

Much of the time is devoted to what adults call play, but which for the child is serious learning-work, through which he learns to know himself, the world of things and people, human relations with his peers and adults, God's love and care. Through action he will learn and express much for which verbal communication is still beyond him. The program suggested in some teachers' guides provides simply for two major elements—free play time and group time—with great flexibility in the portion of the hour devoted to each. A more structured pattern suggests these elements: when the children come, worship suggestions, conversation and relaxation, storytime, related activities, closing. The ability to participate in the group time will increase with each year, and in the course of any one year.

Informal Worship. The responses of young children are characterized by informality and spontaneity. At any point in the program there may be a spontaneous response of awe, wonder, adoration, gratitude, remorse, or love through which the children can be led to turn their thoughts to God in worship. Such times come when the teacher is relating to a single pupil, to a small number of pupils, or to the group as a whole. It may happen in response to a story; observation of a wonderful phenomenon of nature; following an answer to a profound (for the child) question; seeing an object, picture, or scene of beauty; hearing beautiful music; experiencing a joyous event. It may occur in the classroom, in the church sanctuary, or on a nature walk. The movement of the Spirit is not limited by time or place. The time for worship is whenever it is most genuine and meaningful to children.

Teachers should be alert to such opportunities and make them an occasion for worship by relating them to an awareness of God, with a few words, a verse of scripture, a sentence prayer, or the quoting or singing of the words of a familiar hymn. Such moments of spontaneous devotion are not limited to children but can and probably do happen to everyone. But the inhibitions of older pupils make it more difficult for leaders to sense such golden opportunities.

Some leaders of nursery groups feel that this is the only kind of worship of which children of this age are capable. In any case there is no sharp dividing line between this and a period of planned worship at this age. To a lesser extent, this is true also for the kindergarten age.

Planned Worship. Formally planned periods of worship are not a substitute for these spontaneous turnings to God that are experienced by every Christian. However, the practice of Christian churches through the centuries supports the desirability of having God's people assemble at a given time, in a suitable place, with a proper liturgy, for the specific purpose of worship. In simple form such planned worship has a place in the youngest groups. We turn now to a consideration of what form of planned worship is most appropriate for preschool groups.

1. Worship should be an integral part of the class program. Children are not to be moved to another room to meet with other classes, except on special occasions, such as when they join with the congregation in the church sanctuary. In the distinction suggested above between free activity and group time (sometimes also called "quiet time") worship will be included in the latter.

2. One area of the room should be arranged as the place for the quiet time. The focal point of this area will be the "special" table (worship center)—a low table suitably covered and simply furnished. What is placed on this table will provide a setting for the thoughts and attitudes which are contemplated for this period. Concrete suggestion and beauty will be the objective in the table arrangement, rather than symbolic significance. The arrangement will vary with the theme, and may from time to time include a picture, a Bible, flowers, an object of wonder and beauty, candles (for pleasure in their beauty, not as symbolic of some abstract truth). Children and leaders may be seated on a rug or in chairs suitably arranged in relation to the worship center.

3. Children will readily learn that a given musical signal calls them to gather for quiet time. Not all the nursery children may want to join in this or remain in the group throughout the period. There should be no compulsion beyond friendly persuasion. With advancing age, the kindergarten children will be increasingly capable of disciplining themselves to accept the established routine.

Once the children are settled for quiet time, the teacher should find some natural way to lead into worship. Phoebe

Anderson gives an illustration of how this was done with a nursery group at the beginning of the year. The teacher engaged them in conversation about themselves, about babies, how they had grown from babies into three-year-olds, about three-year-olds in the church. She then had them dramatize how they had grown up from babyhood.

> Then Mrs. Kaufman had them all sit down cross-legged in front of her again and she said, "Every Sunday morning when we come to the rug for our story and song and cracker we also say a prayer. When I say a prayer I bow my head and close my eyes and am as quiet as can be.
>
> "Dear God, we are glad we have grown big enough to come to church school. Amen."
>
> Several children bowed their heads and closed their eyes during the prayer.[1]

4. The order of service should be simple, flexible, allow for informality in accepting pupil responses and contributions, and varied to suit the occasion. Florence Schulz writes:

> Opportunities should be presented to the children to respond consciously and articulately to the revelations that God is making on their level of understanding. They need practice, too, in putting their vague knowledge of God into words. And they need to recognize in other human beings—teachers, parents, friends—echoes of their own groping thoughts and feelings.[2]

The same author suggests that the progression of the worship experience might be as follows: a feeling of human

[1] Phoebe M. Anderson, *3's in the Christian Community* (Philadelphia: United Church Press, 1960), p. 43.

[2] Florence Schulz, *Living in the Christian Community* (Philadelphia: United Church Press, 1962), p. 46.

companionship; a reminder of God; a meditation on the reminder of God; a song of praise, a thankful response, or a prayer for help and understanding; a benediction song.[3] The elements which are included in the service are not very different from those in any liturgy, but very different with respect to simplicity and brevity: music, song, prayer, scripture, story, conversation, actions, moments of quiet, offering (not necessarily all in any one service).

5. Songs and hymns which are appropriate for the age-group and for a given theme are suggested in every good leader's manual. Leaders should have copies of one or more good hymnals prepared for use in the department they are leading. See chapter 11 for suggestions.

> The songs will be short and should deal with ideas that are within the experience of the children. Most two- and three-year-old children do not sing many songs themselves. No attempt should be made to drill them on the songs. The teacher will do the singing, but as the songs are used again and again, the children will often learn them from their repeated meaningful use. Sometimes the teacher may ask, "Can you sing it with me?" Often a child will join in all or part of a meaningful song. Parents should be encouraged to sing the nursery songs with their children at home.[4]

6. Bible material suitable for young children is greatly limited. Some feel that only two stories are suitable for nursery—the story of Jesus' birth and Jesus and the children. Others would include somewhat more. Single short verses may be used which express experiences in words, such as "He has made everything beautiful" (Eccles. 3:11); "The earth is the Lord's" (1 Cor. 10:26); "O give thanks

---

[3] *Ibid.*

[4] *Bible Storytime Series,* Year I Nursery Teacher's Guide (Minneapolis: Augsburg, 1957), p. 19. Used by permission of Augsburg Publishing House.

to the Lord, for he is good" (Ps. 106:1); "Be still, and know that I am God" (Ps. 46:10), which may be used as a call to a moment of reverent silence. Since the verses are taken out of context, it should not be assumed that such use has great value as Bible study. That is not the purpose. When used in relation to experience they do help to communicate the meaning of the Bible, and help the pupils to appreciate that it is a very special book for Christians.

Here is an example of using a Bible verse in the context of a group-time setting. After a story about love in family relationships and an appropriate song:

> Open the Bible and say, "There is a very important verse in our Bible that we heard last week. It says, 'Let us love one another.' Can you say it with me as we begin our prayer?" If you have changed your own manner of speaking to quiet thoughtful tones, if you bow your head and fold your hands, the children will sense your attitude and will know that you want to pray. Offer a prayer of thanks for families where we love and care for one another. Express appreciation and wonder at God's plan for babies. Then sing reverently "God Bless Our Home with Love."[5]

The significance of the Bible in preschool Christian education goes beyond its limited verbal use. Its spirit and truth are basic to the whole program, but we want to avoid overburdening children with words they cannot understand in the mistaken notion that such verbal learning is the essence of Christian nurture. The truth of the Bible will be taught in many ways, by actions as well as by words. It will be expressed through stories, pictures, hymns, and deeds. The basis for understanding that God is love is ex-

---

[5] Norma E. Koenig, *Trusting God's Creative Love* (Philadelphia: United Church Press, 1961), p. 111.

perience with persons who love. The teacher's own appreciation of the Bible will be communicated through his attitudes and relationships.

7. Prayers will be brief and natural, and seek to express the children's own inner thoughts and attitudes. They may be related to conversations, stories, and activities. They will be addressed to God, not to Jesus. They will pick up and put into words the pupils' sentiments of awe, gladness and sorrow, gratitude, need for strength and security, a sense of the miracle of creation and life—not in the abstract but in relation to concrete experiences. Leaders should make sure that they are speaking to God for themselves and their children, not using prayer as a means of subtle suggestion of what the children ought to think, feel, and do. The genuineness of the leader's own prayer experience will be reflected in the children.

Usually the prayer will be freely formulated and spoken by the leader. At times the children may share in building a group prayer. Norma Koenig gives an illustration of this in a kindergarten department:

> Suggest that the children fold their hands and think about God's good world. If they would like to say some of the thank-you thoughts aloud, their words can be a prayer for all the group. Begin by thanking God for his nearness. Tell him that the children are thinking about his good care for all living things and that some may want to thank him. Then pause to let the children add to the prayer. If there is silence, address individual children. "Glen, are you thinking about something in God's world?" "Doris, would you like to say thank you for something you have seen today?" But do not insist that they contribute. A nod or a smile may be their only response. The important thing is to let them sense your own informal companionship and love for

God so that they begin to feel they can talk to him in their own way whenever they want to.[6]

Form prayers, spoken in unison, may be used occasionally, provided they are not just meaningless words. They may help the child acquire a prayer vocabulary and, if they fit the occasion, may give him the words to express what he thinks and feels. They should of course be brief, and if they are in rhyme they will be more easily learned. It is doubtful whether preschool children are ready to use the Lord's Prayer with any adequate understanding.

8. If an offering is included as a part of worship, it may be placed in a plate or basket when the children arrive and simply dedicated at the appropriate place in the service. As soon as they are able to understand, children should be taught the meaning of stewardship of money—that Christians bring offerings in thankfulness to God for his love and as a means to help carry on his work. One could argue that the giving of an offering should wait until its meaning can be understood, for young children may get weird notions as to who gets the money. But it is such common practice for children of all ages to bring an offering that the only practical alternative is to try to help them understand the meaning of the act.

9. The reality of worship for children is not measured by the facility with which they can go through certain exercises like so many automatons, but by the genuineness of their communion with God. The attitudes (reverent quiet), actions (bowed heads, rhythmic movements), and materials (recited or sung), which are a means to this, are necessary. But the learning and use of these means should not be confused with the end for which they are used.

---

[6] *Ibid.*, p. 101.

131

Mrs. Koenig has pointed out that some worship periods are little different from the game "Simon Says":

> Simon says, "Stand up." Simon says, "Sit down. Sing a song. Bow your head." Is your group worship just a game of "Simon Says" to the children? Be honest with yourself. How is it different? Unless the children understand what they are doing and respond joyously and willingly, it may not be different at all.[7]

By way of contrast, here is an example of worship which seeks to build on meaningful experience. After seeing pictures, hearing a story, and talking about helpers in the kindergarten group, the teacher said:

> "There are all sorts of helpers, aren't there? Everybody who works is a helper. God planned it this way—that people should help one another. When people work they are really being God's helpers." [Then she] folded her hands in her lap quietly. "Let us sit very still for a minute and think about helpers: the policeman who helps us cross the street, the truck driver who hauls loads for us, the garageman who fixes our cars. I'd like to say, 'Thank you, God, for helpers. We're glad for people who help us. Amen.' And now let's all sing very softly 'Friends! Friends! Friends!' "[8]

---

[7] *Ibid.,* p. 77.

[8] Christina T. Owen, *Helping One Another* (Philadelphia: United Church Press, 1962), p. 19.

9 PRIMARY AND JUNIOR DEPARTMENTS

This chapter deals with worship in the Christian education of boys and girls in the elementary school age—school grades one to six. In the church school they may be classified in two departments of three years each, in three departments of two years each, or by single grades. There is of course a vast difference between a six-year-old and an eleven-year-old child. Throughout these years there is continuous and rapid growth in understanding and ability to use the forms and materials through which worship comes to expression, though not necessarily in the genuineness of the experience itself. There are therefore differences also between the worship activities of the younger and older departments in this six-year span, which will be noted.

THE PUPILS

Basic factors in the children's capacity to worship are what the children are and what their experience of life has been. Their world, which has heretofore been largely confined to the home, the immediate community, and the church kindergarten, is expanding in everwidening circles to include peer groups, club and play groups, relationships with adults outside the home, and a growing sense of belonging to and participating in the Christian fellowship of the church.

At the beginning of this period the boys and girls are entering the exciting new world of school (some of course will have been in public school kindergarten during the previous year). Leaders in the church school can get a good deal of insight in understanding their pupils through visits to the public school for observation of their performance in that setting, including the intellectual level, interest range, and social maturity at which they are able to work. The growing ability to read opens new worlds to the pupils and prepares the way for new methods in the church school.

Preoccupation with the here and now is being tempered with a new sense of time and the ability to think in terms of past events and persons. Reading, television, and the movies are a fruitful source for new experiences in fact and fiction. They serve to acquaint these pupils with critical world events, developments in science and technology, spacecraft and spacemen, war and social conflict. This may result not only in understanding and stimulation but may serve also to arouse fears and anxieties.

The pilgrimage of growth toward maturity moves from dependence on adults toward greater independence, from one-to-one peer relationships to larger groups, from imagination and fancy to fact and reason, from the concrete and objective to an increasing ability to grasp abstract concepts and symbolism, from dependence on others for moral authority to an inner sense of right and wrong and the demands of justice.

If worship—and Christian education in general—is to be relevant to life, leaders must be very much aware of the characteristics, capacities, interests, and activities of the boys and girls they are leading. Some of the best resources for such understanding, and indispensable guides to appropriate forms and materials for a given age-group, are the teachers' manuals of the curriculum. I use the word indispensable advisedly, for only as plans for worship grow out of the total learning setting can it be a climax of the whole experience and not just an unrelated element in the program. Further resources for more extensive study will be found in many books on the understanding of children and their development.

But "book learning" is not enough. Leaders should know their children not just from descriptions in books but as actual living persons. A writer can describe the characteristics of children by age-groups, but the fact remains that actual children never fit such classified descriptions perfectly, for they do not develop by the psychologist's charts, but as individual persons.

THE PROGRAM

With advancement into and through the grades there will usually be a sharper distinction between worship and class-teaching than has been the case in preschool. However, the two should continue to be closely interrelated, and constitute a single curriculum, so that in the experience of worship the religious depth and meaning of church school courses may come to their most significant expression.

In most church schools an abrupt change is made in the

program when children enter the first grade. Whereas in the kindergarten they participated in an informal program in their own classroom which included worship, now they are included in a scheduled service with the whole primary department. Yet there is no abrupt change in the child himself. It would be better if this transition could be made gradually, with the class type of total program continuing at least in the early grades.

Variety of Worship Occasions. Grade school children need not be limited to one type of worship experience. It is desirable that they have an opportunity to share in the several types which have previously been described. Which type will predominate must depend on many factors in the local church, and to a large extent on the age of the pupils, with progressive advancement toward the more formal type of service.

1. Worship within the class need not be excluded at any age, and may predominate in the earlier grades. Such periods for worship may be placed at almost any point in the program, but are preferably scheduled near the end of the class period, so that they may include thoughts and events which may have developed in the session. At the appropriate time the pupils will be seated in a designated section of the room, facing a simple interest table or worship center. Conversation about what has gone before may be directed to a thought or theme around which the service will be developed. The plan for the service may be quite brief and informal. A general pattern for this is suggested in the following section. If the pupils have a share in arranging the room and planning and conducting the service, it will heighten their interest and appreciation.

Teachers will continue to encourage moments of spontaneous worship as opportunities present themselves at any point in class activity. The nature of this kind of experience was described in the preceding chapter. The following example is from a course for first and second grades:

"How can it be that we grow and not feel ourselves growing?" asked Mary, who seemed to voice a question felt by the others in the group. After several moments of silent wonder, the teacher turned to the verse on the chart and the group read aloud: "This is the Lord's doing; it is marvelous in our eyes."

The sensitive teacher may guide moments of wonder into an experience of worship by turning the children's thoughts to God. It is impossible to plan when such moments will come, but teachers should continually be alert to capture such times of wonder, awe, or concern.[1]

2. Worship by department groups—occasionally or frequently, as deemed best by the leaders—may also be provided for grade school pupils. While there are distinct values in having class-type worship, there are values also in larger departmental groupings. Corporate worship is an act of God's people—praising him, and in fellowship with each other. Children should learn to sense their fellowship with groups larger than a single class. A service with a larger group, in a more "churchly" setting, can be more like the church service, that is, follow more closely the accepted pattern for public worship, and as a by-product provide a transition to participation in the worship of the congregation.

The grades to be included in the several department groups should correspond to the way the curriculum is

---

[1] Barbara Kinney Hargis, *In the Image of God* (Philadelphia: United Church Press, 1963), p. 34.

organized. Only thus can the experience of worship be integrated with the content of the rest of the curriculum. Hence the departmental organization will provide for two three-year groups (usually named primary and junior) or three two-year groups (primary, lower junior, junior). In large church schools which have two or more classes in each grade, single grades may constitute the departments. This is especially advantageous if closely graded lessons are used.

The department meetings will be held in rooms especially adapted to and arranged for worship (see chapter 7 for suggestions) or in a classroom temporarily arranged for this purpose. Ten to fifteen minutes are sufficient for the service, but additional time will need to be allowed for movement of classes and for training in worship. Hence the church school period should be more than sixty minutes if there is to be adequate time for class sessions.

What has been said above has been on the assumption that a church is able to establish the recognized departments in its organization. There are unfortunately many churches which by reason of small numbers or lack of available rooms need to combine wider age ranges for worship. It is questionable whether a general service for the whole church school is desirable. It would be better to make this a *church* service—either a family-type service or some combination with morning worship—led by the minister, and in the church sanctuary. If an additional room is available the youngest children should have priority in its use.

The more likely situation makes it necessary to combine only two or three departments. In such cases the effort should be made to include in the service something which is in the range of interest and understanding of each of the departments so combined. In such a combined service it is difficult to relate worship to the teaching program in each department, but the effort should be made to find some common elements through which relationship can be established. Leaders will need to be acquainted with the curriculum in each of the departments, and class teachers can help pupils prepare for meaningful participation.

3. Participation in the general church service should be a familiar experience to primary and junior boys and girls, in addition to worship in classes and departments. This may be arranged through regular or occasional family services, through attendance at the regular church service on scheduled Sundays or on special occasions, such as Christmas, Easter, and Church School Sunday. Let us re-emphasize that the mere presence of children in such services in not enough. They should regard themselves as first-class members of a congregation which has gathered to make its offering to God, and so accepted by minister and people.

Orders of Worship. The order of service should have these characteristics: It should be built on a central thought or theme; it should provide a succession of acts through which an experience of the worship of God may be achieved; it should be sufficiently constant in form to assure familiarity and to avoid confusion; it should be varied in form from time to time to avoid monotony and mere mechanical response; it should vary in content to fit the theme.

A leader who understands the principles of public worship will be free to develop his own orders in accordance with what seems to him to accomplish best the purpose of true worship, to be suitable for the age of pupils he is leading, and to be in harmony with the theme for a given service. These designs are offered only by way of suggestion.

In a primary department course the following plan for worship is given as part of the lesson treatment for one of the Sundays. The purpose of the session is stated as: "To observe and wonder with the boys and girls at some of the things in our world that may help us to know God because we see in them evidences of his power and wisdom as the creator." This is the theme for the service that follows:

PRIMARY ORDER OF WORSHIP

Call to Worship: Psalm 107:1 (read from the Bible by the teacher).

Hymn: "Thank Thee, God."

Scripture: Open your Bible to Psalm 107 again and say something like this: "Our Bible helps us to learn about God. Many people have written in it stories and songs telling about God's loving care for his people. Often the writers want to say a special 'thank you' for God's loving care and to remind others to do so also. This is what one writer has said." Read Psalm 107:1. "Another writer says it this way." Read Psalm 105:1-2.

Prayer: Say a brief prayer of thanks to God for all the wonderful things he has made in the world, naming some specific wonders that have most interested the children.

Service of Offering: Follow your customary pattern.

Hymn: "All Things Bright and Beautiful" or "For the Beauty of the Earth."[2]

---

[2] Gertrude Priester, *God Is Love* (Philadelphia: United Church Press, 1963), p. 47.

By the time the children have reached the third or fourth grade, they are ready for a somewhat more elaborate service. An increasing amount of simple liturgical material may be used. The maximum time devoted to actual worship should be not more than ten to fifteen minutes. A few minutes may be added to this for preparing the group for worship, and for training in new materials.

In my leadership of junior groups I prepare an order of service which will be used from four to six weeks, thus allowing the pupils to become familiar with it. This is mimeographed on one side of a single sheet of heavy paper, 5½ x 8½ inches and of an attractive color. The sheets are distributed each Sunday with the hymnbooks. Each week the hymns, scripture, story or talk, and prayer are selected to fit the theme. New hymns are often used several weeks in succession. After a suitable period of weeks a new order is prepared with some changes in the printed responses so as to avoid monotony and enable the pupils to become acquainted with a wider range of liturgical material.

Following is an example. The words in parentheses are not on the pupils' copies but are included here to show how the service was done on a particular Sunday.

JUNIOR ORDER OF WORSHIP

Prelude   Lighting of Candles

Call to Worship

    LEADER: Our help is in the name of the Lord,
                who made heaven and earth.

    PEOPLE: Let the people praise thee, O God,
                Let all the people praise thee.

Prayer of Invocation

Hymn of Praise ("All Creatures of Our God and King")

Scripture (Mark 2:1-12, a story of Jesus' healing ministry. On this occasion read by a pupil.)

Sermon or Story ("One Great Hour of Sharing," including a filmstrip)

Prayer

    LEADER: The Lord be with you.

    PEOPLE: And with thy spirit.

    LEADER: Let us pray . . .

            O Lord, show thy mercy upon us,

    PEOPLE: And grant us thy salvation.

    LEADER: O God, make clean our hearts within us,

    PEOPLE: And take not thy Holy Spirit from us.

    Prayer by the leader, or the Lord's Prayer in unison.
    (On this occasion, a prayer by the leader, related to
    the theme. We do not use the Lord's Prayer every
    Sunday lest it become a mere meaningless form.)

Offering

    LEADER: Remember the words of our Lord Jesus,
            how he said:

    PEOPLE: It is more blessed to give than to receive.

    Collection and Presentation of the Offering

    The Doxology

Hymn ("We Would See Jesus")

Benediction

    IN UNISON: May the words that we say,

              and the thoughts that we pray,

              stay with us and help us,

              this day and always. Amen.

Postlude   Extinguishing of Candles

Comments on Elements in the Order of Service. Little
need be added to what has been said in chapter 3 concern-

ing the elements which constitute the order of service, except to indicate how some of them are used with primary and junior boys and girls.

1. The *message* may be in the form of a story, sermon, guided conversation, or visual presentation (a picture on which an oral presentation is focused, a filmstrip which tells a story, and so forth). Although an appropriate story is the most common vehicle for the message, we know from experience that children will listen to and profit by a talk (sermon) if it is made brief, concrete, and within their vocabulary and experience. The message should highlight the theme and give meaning and direction to the whole service. If the theme has already been consciously established in prior class activity a brief reminder may be all that is needed.

2. *Hymns* and music are a great aid to joy in worship. In the younger grades a song chart in large print will serve to focus the attention. After initial interpretation, the words will be learned through use rather than by drill. By the middle of this age span pupils will be able to use hymnals. The nature and use of a hymnal should be explained when pupils are first introduced to it. Enough copies of the hymnal should be available so that each pupil may have one. Hymnals specifically prepared for a given department are the best guide to hymns which are appropriate for that age. Leaders will need to keep a balance between repeating a few familiar hymns and exposing pupils more widely to the rich resources of our hymnody. An increasing number of the great hymns of the church can and should be used as pupils advance through these grades.

Some understanding of the words of hymns is essential if they are to be used with meaning, but not necessarily complete understanding. There are few church hymns

143

which do not have concepts and allusions that will not be clearly understood until later.

3. "The *Bible* is read so that the congregation together may praise God and hear his word to them . . . in order that God's people may be reminded both of his promises and of how they can serve him."[3] It has also provided us with liturgical responses and the basis for a central theme. In younger grades, passages need to be brief and concrete in meaning. Bible stories may be retold to make them more comprehensible, but with care that the retold story is faithful to the meaning of its scriptural source. After pupils have their own Bibles and have learned to use them with some facility, they may join in unison reading.

It is good practice to have the church, or the church and the parents jointly, present Bibles to pupils at the age when they are ready to use them. This is a concrete way of recognizing their growth in the fellowship and their ability for larger participation. It is also a practical way to assure that all will have the same version (which should be the Revised Standard Version). The appropriate time for this presentation will normally be at the beginning of the fourth or fifth grade, depending on whether the curriculum is organized by three-year or two-year departments.

One of the perennial questions of church school workers is whether there should be memory work, and if so, how to get it done. Memorization for its own sake of materials which have little present meaning is of doubtful value. But to furnish the mind with great passages of scripture and hymns, which express deep thoughts in more sublime and beautiful words than our own, is a means to great enrich-

---

[3] Iris V. Cully, *Children in the Church* (Philadelphia: Westminster Press, 1960), copyright © by W. L. Jenkins, p. 185. Used by permission.

ment of life. As they mature, the pupils will find deeper meaning in the passages they have memorized. One of the best opportunities for memorization is in relation to the program of worship. It provides the proper conditions for memorization—worthy materials, opportunity for use in a natural setting, meaningful repetition through frequent use. The service of worship will acquaint the pupil with scripture, prayers, hymns, responses, which are worthy of being carried in memory as a lifelong possession. He may not be able to recite many of these out of context, but if mastery to that level is desired it can be accomplished with a minimum of additional study and drill in classes and at home.

4. *Prayers* which are appropriate and meaningful are for most leaders the point of greatest difficulty in leading worship. To be genuine prayer, thoughts must be directed to conversation with God and expressed in words that can be accepted by the pupils as their own. The content may include something which the group has experienced together, but it is more than a conversation between leader and pupils about that experience. There is a language appropriate to prayer, yet the leader needs to avoid meaningless and trite words and expressions. He must probe the genuine sentiments of the boys and girls and not just project thoughts on them that they may not sense at all. All of which is to say that the prayer in the service deserves a good deal of prayerful preparation on the leader's part.

Form prayers may be used, provided they are carefully selected for meaning and relevance. Older boys and girls can make appreciative use of some of the great classical prayers. Suggestions for worship in leaders' guides usually include prayers, but until these are rethought and reworked so as to become the leader's own prayer thoughts, they are not likely to be effective. One means of involving the pupils more fully is to have them contribute their own thoughts to a group prayer. See pages 130-31 for an example of this.

5. The *offering* will increase in significance as response to God during the primary and junior years. Boys and girls can collect the offering and bring it to the chancel for dedication. They will not only appreciate this opportunity for participation but perform the service in a dignified manner if given some initial coaching. Education in the meaning of Christian giving, in a setting of the stewardship of all of life, will be a continuing part of training for worship. As they grow in their sense of being a part of the whole church fellowship, the pupils will appreciate having a part in its work through contributing to the church budget. Regular and systematic giving should be encouraged through the use of offering envelopes.

Offerings for special projects which appeal to children, such as One Great Hour of Sharing, may be planned from time to time. In this, however, care must be exercised to avoid a patronizing attitude of giving to "the poor," "the unfortunate," "the Negro children at Hope Mission," and so on. Giving should be in a spirit of friendship and sharing with those who are just as worthy as we.

6. *Pupil participation* in the worship service is desirable. Worship should be *with* pupils and not *for* them. Pupils may help in planning the service and in arranging the setting for it. On a rotation basis they may serve as doorkeepers, ushers, acolytes, deacons, and so forth. Occasionally a class in the department may plan and conduct the entire service, provided that their teacher has sufficient sense of what worship involves to guide them in planning. Now and then an individual pupil may be designated to

read the scripture or take some other part, but favoritism in choosing only the best readers and speakers is to be avoided. The desire to have pupils participate in leadership should not be allowed to overbalance the need for a dignified and worshipful service.

But above everything else, let us remember that to guide an experience of worship is a highly developed art which demands the mature skill of an adult. Under trained adult guidance children may feel that they are participating freely and democratically in a service of worship to which they have made creative contributions, even though an adult, not a child, does the actual leading. But, since we are seeking to maintain balance in our program-building, let us make a place for those occasional services through which the boys and girls share some meaningful experience with others in the group or some group invited in to worship with them.[4]

---

[4] Marie Cole Powell, *Boys and Girls at Worship* (New York: Harper & Row, 1943), p. xviii.

10 YOUTH AND ADULTS

The place of worship in the Christian education of youth and adults can be treated more briefly than in the case of children because for these groups the corporate worship of the church will be the chief center of their worship life. Also by virtue of their maturity, worship activities in their own groups require less adaptation in form and content from that which characterizes worship in general.

Let us not assume, however, that worship can now be given a secondary role. Religious learning is not something added to life; it permeates the whole of existence with meaning in relation to life under God. Through worship the intellectual understanding of the nature of God, prayer, justification by faith, Christian ethics in personal and social relations, take on a new dimension in personal experience of communion with God, faith, and commitment.

WORSHIP FOR YOUTH

For the purpose of this discussion we are designating as youth all young people who are in school grades seven to twelve, or are ages twelve to eighteen in case of those who have dropped out of school. In the small church school they may be organized as a single youth department, but it is better to have two departments: junior high school and high school; or three departments: junior high, middle high, and high school.

This is a period of transition from childhood to early maturity. The youth enter this period as children who have been largely dependent on adult authority; they leave it as more or less self-directive persons. It is a period of tremendous new experience and learning. At some point during these years the young people will undergo confirmation and admission to communicant membership in the church. Our present concern is: How may worship be a vital factor in interpreting and shaping these tremendous experiences of youth?

Who Are These Youth? Those who are called to lead youth in worship will realize that this involves more than teaching them to participate in outward forms, but that true worship springs from their inner nature and being. Basic to such leadership is an understanding of the young people as persons. John G. Williams has pointed out:

> The immense importance of adolescence is that, where development is allowed to follow a healthy course, the young person is, by the very laws of his unfolding nature, searching for the things we most want him to find in Christian worship. . . . [These include] the three basic needs of the adolescent as he tries to find a purpose for his life: (1)

someone to trust; (2) something to belong to; (3) something to live for.

It is revealing to study the ways in which the totalitarian movements of our time have succeeded in capturing the allegiance of young people on sound psychological lines by an appeal to those three fundamental needs.[1]

Youth are in a time of breaking away from authority and seeking an authentic self-identity. They are strongly influenced by the culture of the peer group, yet long for acceptance by the larger society. They are confronted with perplexities, problems, anxieties, incident to growing up. They are extremely conscious of the other sex and seeking to find viable relationships. They are frequently in rebellion, not always for rebellion's sake, but as a necessary road to achieving mature selfhood. Before the end of high school most of them will have wrestled with problems of career, leaving school or higher education, the choice of a marriage partner (perhaps only in its initial stages), and the place they will accord the church in their lives.

The Program. Worship will be an integral part of the total program, and should be treated in light of this. The capacity for and the desire to enter into worship will increase with movement through the high school grades, but will vary widely with individuals. The full range of the worship experience as adoration, confession, thanksgiving, supplication, submission-commitment, is now within their understanding, and the young people are capable of participating meaningfully in the church liturgy. Following confirmation there will be increasing identification

---

[1] John G. Williams, *Worship and the Modern Child* (London: National Society, S.P.C.K., 1957), pp. 187-88.

with the Christian fellowship and participation in its mission. The young men and women can appropriate the meaning of the priesthood of believers and how this may find expression in ministry to each other and to the world.

An excellent characterization of the thrust of the youth program has been made by Richard L. Harbour:

> Christianity has a mission to the youth culture. It resembles the mission which Christians carry to any other peoples or cultures in that it cannot be effective until those who are under the culture's influence are themselves involved in the mission. It is like the mission to other cultures in that its most effective functions take place via educational channels. The educational function of the mission with youth who are in the church has a difference and an advantage. It can educe, that is, bring or draw forth, that which has been received through revelation, instruction, and discipline prior to and during the adolescent years. Christian education can assist in opening young minds and hearts to the "wideness in God's mercy" and it can introduce them to the fact that "the love of God is broader than the measure of man's mind."[2]

Occasions and Types of Worship. The church's ministry to youth offers a number of settings in which worship may take place, and the opportunity for various types of services each of which may make a contribution to the whole worship life. Chief of these is the general public worship of the congregation. Young people at this age—certainly from the year of confirmation—should make participation with the gathered church their primary occasion for wor-

---

[2] Richard L. Harbour, "Adolescence," *The Westminster Dictionary of Christian Education,* ed. Kendig Brubaker Cully (Philadelphia: Westminster Press, 1963), copyright © 1963 by W. L. Jenkins, p. 7. Used by permission.

ship. Let us not assume, however, that if this is happening the ultimate has been realized.

Enrichment in both experience and understanding can come through age-group services, which may well be less formal, less traditional, more experimental, more sensitive to youth interests, and use materials better adapted to express their thoughts and feelings. At this age the pupils have two abilities (as distinguished from younger children) which affect the types of services planned with them: (1) they can share more fully in the general ritual; (2) they can enter more fully and creatively into the process of planning and conducting the service.

Assuming their attendance at the church service as well as participation in youth groups, there is little need for departmental worship services in the youth departments of the Sunday church school. The junior high department may be an exception to this because the younger age of the pupils may make it desirable to have a service of their own, and the pupils may be less fully involved in church attendance and the youth group. The need for experience and training can better be provided through worship in classes. This should normally take place near the end of the class period so as to make it possible to incorporate and lift to the level of worship some of the thinking and experience which have gone before. This may consist of just a closing prayer, but on occasion may also include music, a hymn, a scripture reading, a poem, or a short meditation. It may be in the charge of a class worship committee. Education in worship should be given as needed, both in relation to the worship itself and through units in the curriculum on the meaning of worship.

In most churches there will be organized youth groups, especially for those who are post-confirmation. Such groups usually include worship as a part of the program, and here the service may be more fully developed than that suggested for the Sunday church school. In relation to the youth ministry there may be retreats, work projects, summer conferences, and other events, which offer unparalleled opportunity for depth experiences. On any of these occasions various types of worship may be planned, such as outdoor vespers, fireside, candlelight, silent meditation, as well as the more traditional form. (See pages 116-17 for suggestions.)

Participation. Pupil participation will be of two kinds: (1) pupils will be involved in the service as their own offering to God in worship, not as spectators to something that the leader is doing to which their response is casual and formal; (2) they will have a large share in planning and leadership. In the church service, pupil participation will be largely of the first kind, but young people should also have a part as ushers, choir members, and liturgists on youth Sundays. The youth groups offer a larger opportunity for pupil leadership.

When pupils assist in planning and leading there is greater possibility that worship will be relevant to their interests and needs. The young people will find expression in forms and materials which for them are effective vehicles to communion with God. Pupils of this age are capable of taking a large share in planning and conducting worship, but in doing this they should have the guidance and counsel of their teachers and department leaders.

Adult Leadership. The function of the adult leader is more that of teaching and training youth in the art of worship than of conducting services for them, although on rare occasion the leader may do the latter. While it is sound practice to let the young people take a large measure of responsibility for the worship aspect of the program, if this results in superficial, careless, or flippant handling of great themes and sublime materials, the purposes of Christian education are not adequately served. However, with guidance and supervision youth are capable of discharging this function in a manner which may even be superior to what the leader himself might do, precisely because their effort comes out of the very life of the group.

During these years there is need for continuing education in the nature and meaning of worship. Younger children will accept almost without question what we give them, but it is the nature of adolescents to be critical and to evaluate in terms of their own thinking. Some may even question whether having worship at all makes any sense. Pupils of this age need to move from passive acceptance of the forms of worship to active seeking and finding, to opening their hearts and minds to God's spirit.

Beyond such basic understanding of the function of worship in life, pupils need to learn (or relearn in light of their increasing maturity) the forms and materials through which the impulse to worship is best realized, both as congregation and as leaders, and within the setting of their own group. Much of this education will be acquired in relation to the experiences of planning, leading, and participating. It will be supported and intensified through units on worship in the curriculum.

It is a function of the adult leader to provide resources for pupil planners and leaders. Some of these will be found in the teachers' and pupils' manuals of the curriculum. Beyond this, pupils will need pamphlets and books on the art of worship, books of suggestions for worship, collections of poems and devotional readings, prayers and other liturgical materials, pictures and projected audio visuals, and so forth. The alert leader will build a file of clippings from newspapers and magazines of incidents, poems, pictures, which may at some future time be found useful. (See chapter 11 for suggested books of resources.)

WORSHIP FOR ADULTS

We are designating as adults all persons who have completed high school and any others who are beyond the high school years. A distinction should be made between young adults, middle-age adults, and older adults. There is no question but that the way in which worship comes to specific expression in these groups, as well as other aspects of their Christian education, varies with their ages. But the general character of worship for all of them is sufficiently similar to make it unnecessary to treat them separately here.

Whatever may be the case with respect to children and youth, the primary occasion for worship of all adults is the church service. In large part, adults are the worshiping congregation. If their worship needs are not met in this service, the answer is not in giving them a substitute. It is in improving such services to meet their needs more fully and in educating them in better understanding and greater appreciation. What is done by way of worship in the adult departments must be on the assumption that these same men and women are regular participants in the corporate worship of the church.

Adult Worship in the Church School. If the above is accepted as a basic principle in the Christian education of

155

adults, the question may be raised whether any other provision for worship should be made for them. If adults *are* the worshiping congregation, is there any need for worship in adult groups? Our answer to this question is affirmative in view of the following considerations:

1. The study of the Bible and other Christian subjects should be in a devotional spirit and lead naturally into expression in worship. If worship is not a constant companion of study, the class activity will not eventuate in the highest outcome in personal appropriation and commitment.

2. Adults are not beyond the need for education in worship. The church school must take the responsibility for this, since such education cannot well be given in the church service. We should perhaps be able to assume that when persons have reached adulthood they will have acquired an understanding of public worship and the ability to respond through the acts of the liturgy. For many this is not the case. All need continuing growth in worship and the devotional life, or, as Robert Koenig has warned, "they will become trapped in the forms of ritual instead of being confronted in worship by God's claim on their lives."[3]

As in other church school groups, education will be related to leadership of and participation in class or department worship activities and enriched through units on worship in the curriculum. One aspect of this training is to help laymen become proficient in public prayer. It is a tragic fact that in many congregations there are few lay-

[3] Robert E. Koenig, "Learning to Worship Is a Developing Process," *Church School Worker*, July-August, 1961, p. 15.

men who consider themselves competent to lead in prayer —at least not when the minister is present.

3. Whatever may be the ideal, there are in every church some adults who for reasons of their own do not attend the church services. This may be especially true of young adults. Yet they may participate in other adult activities. For them, worship in such other groups should serve a peculiar need, and it may also help in building a bridge to participation in worship with the congregation as a whole.

Occasions and Types of Worship. Whenever people gather as church groups, in the name of the Lord, to study his word and to do his work, there is an occasion for worship. The form which this takes may vary from a simple prayer to a more elaborate service.

1. In the Sunday church school, which usually immediately precedes the church service, no extended period of worship is necessary or desirable. Maximum time should be reserved for study and discussion, which is the primary purpose of adult church school groups. Classes may open with a brief devotional period or close with a short meditation on some of the thoughts and materials that have been of greatest concern. Such periods of worship may include prayer, devotional reading of scripture, other devotional material, a hymn (either read or sung), a meditation. If there is an assembly of adult classes, a few minutes may be devoted to worship, but brevity and informality will still be the rule with no thought of duplicating the church service.

2. In the case of adult study groups which meet at some time during the week the same suggestions will apply with respect to worship, except that more time may be devoted

to it. This is suggested because they are not held in close relation to the church service, and usually have more time for their sessions than is the case on Sunday morning. Let it be emphasized, however, that worship is included in such meetings because it serves a genuine purpose. It is not just a perfunctory formality.

3. Besides study groups there are meetings of adults which may include worship as part of their activities, such as women's and men's groups, couples clubs, neighborhood groups, boards, and committees. In all too many instances worship in such groups is a mere formality, poorly planned and sloppily conducted. It would be better to omit it entirely than to perpetrate such a travesty. Yet these meetings can be made occasions of genuine worship through careful preparation by the leader of himself and of the group.

The following quotation is an excellent retrospect of the point of view on the place of worship in the Christian education of adults which we have sought to develop in the preceding pages:

> Adults, in their response to God, are moved to praise and gratitude. These are basic elements of worship. Adults are also called to a constant search for a more meaningful and a more perfect witness to the new life that God has given; this involves searching and learning. In all of their activities whether in praise or thanksgiving, in study or in work, they are involved in worship. In this sense all of life is a prayer.[4]

---

[4] Walter E. Dobler, *Manual for Adults* (Philadelphia: United Church Press, 1963), p. 57.

11 RESOURCES FOR
WORSHIP LEADERS

Like any other competent workman, the leader of worship needs first to have a basic understanding of his craft and then to have readily available the materials and tools with which to do his work.

Leading worship is an art, and preparing to lead requires creative activity. True worship is not likely to result from the mechanical use of a prepared order of worship, any more than effective teaching can be done with the use of a lesson plan prepared for the teacher by the lesson writer. In both cases there are factors inherent in the setting, the occasion, the particular pupils, the leader or teacher, and the purpose for the particular group, which make it necessary that the plan be creatively designed to serve best in the particular situation.

This is by way of saying that the needs of leaders will not be served by giving them ready-made services which they can use with little effort—much as some of them would like to have this done. If they are to lead a group with sincerity and power it must be through a vehicle which has been internalized as their very own. Suggested orders of worship are helpful as guides, and at times a prepared service may be used because it accords exactly with what the leader himself would like to do. But usually such services need to be modified for a particular leader's use.

It follows, then, that leaders of worship should have a library of resources available to them on which they can draw as need requires. In this chapter an attempt is made to suggest some of these resources, but more important, to indicate what kinds of materials are useful and where they may be found. The sources for materials are so vast and varied that only a "such as" list can be made. The availability of anything suggested will vary for different leaders according to their particular denominational publications, their access to church and public libraries, and their ability to purchase books and other materials for their personal libraries.

For purposes of identification the publishers of the books listed will be given. Readers should understand that any of the books may be purchased from the supply houses of their own denominations. Most of them will be found in the catalog of such agencies, with description and price.

Some of the titles are out of print, as indicated, but they are listed because the books may still be available at bookstores and at church and public libraries.

THE UNDERSTANDING OF WORSHIP

In previous chapters an attempt has been made to give church school leaders an understanding of the nature and meaning of worship as a basis for intelligent planning for their particular groups, but this has of necessity been brief. Some leaders will want to go beyond this to more intensive study. Dozens of books have been published that might serve this purpose. No doubt your minister has some of these in his library and will gladly recommend the ones he considers best and loan them to you. The following materials have been most helpful:

Brenner, Scott Francis. *The Art of Worship:* A Guide in Corporate Worship Techniques. New York: Macmillan Co., 1961. Included is an appendix which has a glossary of liturgical terms that should be especially useful to laymen.

Hedley, George P. *When Protestants Worship.* Nashville: Abingdon Press, 1961. This was published for the Cooperative Publication Association as a text for an elective course for young adults. Among the strong features that recommend this book is the section of several chapters devoted to the historical development of public worship.

Williams, John G. *Worship and the Modern Child.* London: National Society, S.P.C.K. (New York: Seabury Press), 1957. This book deals broadly with the religious life of the child (including adolescents) in the home and in the church. It is addressed primarily to the British situation but, in spite of some differences in terminology and context, should be useful to American readers.

Brown, Edgar S., Jr. *Living the Liturgy.* Philadelphia: Fortress Press, 1961. Designed as a guide to the Lutheran liturgy, this book seeks to help the churchgoer to understand and appreciate the form of worship which from early times has been the Christian's chief act of response to God.

Fauth, Robert T. *When We Worship.* Philadelphia: United Church Press, 1961. This book is concerned with the elements of worship in the church and emphasizes music, the sacraments, and the order of worship. It is helpful in understanding the meanings and values of worship.

Cully, Kendig Brubaker (ed.). *The Westminster Dictionary of Christian Education*. Philadelphia: Westminster Press, 1963. Articles on worship, various aspects of liturgy, and understanding of pupils of different ages are helpful for worship leaders.

Filmstrips that are useful in education of pupils for worship include: *Christians Worship, Our Service of Worship, One God* ("Ways We Worship in America Series"), *Kathy Finds Ways to Worship, Planning for Worship* ("Planning Better Youth Meetings" Kit), *Christian Symbols*. Consult your audio-visual catalog for descriptions and prices.

GENERAL RESOURCES

Some general aids to worship should be available to leaders, including suggested orders of service and materials for use in worship.

The Bible. Suggested are the Revised Standard Version, if this is used in the church school, and one or more alternate versions, such as *The New English Bible: New Testament* and the translations by J. B. Phillips.

A Concordance. This is a valuable aid in locating passages of scripture that the leader may desire to use.

The Church Hymnal that is used in the general church services.

A Service Book or manual of public worship. While such manuals are planned for use with adult congregations, some of the prayers, responses, litanies, calls to worship, and benedictions will be found suitable also for use with older children and youth. The following are examples of service books: *A Book of Worship for Free Churches,* prepared under the direction of the General Council of the Congregational Christian Churches; *Book of Worship* or *The Hymnal,* published for the Evangelical and Reformed Church; *The Book of Common Worship,* approved by the General Assembly of the Presbyterian Church in the U.S.A.; *The Book of Common Prayer,* according to the use of the Protestant Episcopal Church in the U.S.A.; *Christian Worship, A Service Book,* edited by G. Edwin Osborn, published by the Christian Board of Publication (Christian Churches); *The Book of Worship for Church and Home* (Methodist).

Anthologies of materials for use in worship—poems, prayers, devotional readings, art interpretations, hymns and their interpretation and history. Following are a few which the writer has found useful:

Paine, Howard, and Thompson, Bard. *Book of Prayers for Church and Home.* Philadelphia: United Church Press, 1962. This book has a generous, wide-ranging collection of prayers and litanies from the devotional treasure of the Christian church. A total of 416 entries represent both ancient and modern liturgies.

Maus, Cynthia Pearl. *Christ and the Fine Arts* (rev. ed.). New York: Harper & Row, 1959. This book contains reproductions in black and white of one hundred famous art pictures, with interpretations and appropriate hymns, stories, and poems. Color transparencies of the pictures for projection may be purchased from a denominational supply house. Also by the same author, and of a similar nature, are *The World's Great Madonnas, The Old Testament and the Fine Arts,* and *The Church and the Fine Arts.*

Bailey, Albert E. *The Gospel in Hymns.* New York: Charles Scribner's Sons, 1950. The stories of hymns and hymn writers, with interpretation of the words of the hymns, are found in this book.

Bowman, Clarice M. *Resources for Worship.* New York: Association Press, 1961. Part 1 deals with the nature and practice of worship, and with worship in various groups and on various occasions; part 2 contains resources classified by seventeen themes.

MacKay, Ruth. *They Sang a New Song.* Nashville: Abingdon Press, 1959. This book has stories of twenty great hymns, all suitable for children, with illustrations, words, and music. The type size and illustrations make it suitable for reading by children.

Rest, Friedrich. *Worship Services for Church Groups.* Philadelphia: United Church Press, 1962. A collection of aids for informal worship in church and related groups of all ages and in various situations is given. The opening chapters deal with why we worship and offer suggestions for worship leaders.

Rest, Friedrich. *Our Christian Symbols.* Philadelphia: United Church Press, 1954. The book interprets more than one hundred symbols. It is illustrated.

AGE-GROUP RESOURCES

Curriculum Materials. The most useful resource for planning and conducting worship in departments and classes of the several age-groups is the curriculum material. Every good curriculum includes suggestions for worship as a part of the lesson treatments. Only as worship is related to this whole will it be most meaningful. The theme for worship grows out of the purpose and content of the entire session. Scripture, prayers, hymns, pictures, story, relate to the whole learning experience. Hymns that are particularly pertinent but may not be included in most hymnals are in some cases printed in the curriculum materials. Suggested orders of service are usually given but will generally need to be recast for most effective use by the local leader and group. For older pupils, the students' manuals may include some worship materials.

Leaders of worship who are not also teaching classes should acquaint themselves with the plans and materials for the entire session as a background for their own planning. To avoid upsetting the teachers' plans, stories which are intended for use in class should not be used in the worship service unless such use has been cleared with the teachers. When several classes, which use different courses, are grouped together, the leader will still try to find some common elements that relate to the class sessions, although this is more difficult than is the case when all classes use the same course.

Hymn books should be selected in accordance with the recommendation of the denomination. Suggestions for this will usually be included in the leaders' guides of the curriculum. Leaders of groups in which the pupils do not yet use hymnals will need at least two copies each of one or more hymnals designed for their particular departments. The following are some of the hymnals most widely in use:

NURSERY AND KINDERGARTEN: *Songs for Early Childhood; Songs for the Nursery School* by Laura P. MacCarteney; *Martin and Judy Songs* by Edith Lovell Thomas; *Sing for Joy* by Norman and Margaret Mealy.

PRIMARY: *Songs for Little People* by Frances W. Danielson and Grace W. Conant, *The Whole World Singing* by Edith Lovell Thomas, *Sing for Joy* by Norman and Margaret Mealy.

JUNIOR: *Hymns for Junior Worship; Singing Worship with Boys and Girls* and *The Whole World Singing* by Edith Lovell Thomas. Juniors may also use a general church school hymnal, such as *Sing to the Lord* (United Church Press), which includes some of the best hymns of the church; a youth hymnal; or the church hymnal.

YOUTH AND ADULTS: A good general church school hymnal; *The Hymnal for Youth;* the church hymnal.

Other Aids. Most leaders will want other resources in addition to those in the curriculum. Suggested worship services, graded by departments beginning with primary, are a regular monthly feature in the *International Journal of Religious Education* and in some denominational publications. There are also books which seek to meet this need. Only a few books can be listed here. Consult your denominational supply catalog for additional titles.

PRIMARY: Brown, Jeanette Perkins. *Children's Worship in the Church School.* New York: Harper & Row, 1939. Also by the same author, to help leaders in planning worship, are *As Children Worship* (Philadelphia: United Church Press, 1936) and *More Children's Worship in the Church School* (out of print).

JUNIOR: Bays, Alice A., and Oakberg, Elizabeth J. *Worship Programs for Juniors.* Nashville: Abingdon Press, 1960.

YOUTH: Bailey, J. Martin and Betty Jane. *Worship with Youth.* Philadelphia: United Church Press, 1962. Part 1 deals with planning worship; part 2 gives resources.

Barclay, William. *Epilogues and Prayers.* Nashville: Abingdon Press, 1963. This book includes one hundred brief worship services for youth.

Couch, Helen F., and Barefield, Sam S. *Worship Sourcebook for Youth.* Nashville: Abingdon Press, 1962. This includes materials for use in worship on all sorts of occasions, not primarily in the church school.

Story Resources. "Where can I find suitable stories for worship?" is a question frequently asked by leaders. In answering this question we must first point out that not every service requires a story. The message may often be presented by other means. Second, since the theme for worship should relate to the whole session, the first place to look is in the materials of the curriculum. Beyond this, many of the resources which have been listed above include stories. Creative leaders will be on the alert for incidents reported in the daily press and elsewhere that may be developed into suitable stories; a file of clippings may be an invaluable aid. Sometimes short incidents that are just right for a given purpose can be lifted out of longer stories in books and magazines. Creativity in making or adapting his own stories to suit an occasion is a valuable asset in the art of the storyteller.

There are few books in which a leader can find many stories that are suitable for his own purpose. Several books are suggested below in which he may find some selections that he can use, in some cases with adaptations.

CHILDREN: Fahs, Sophia L. *From Long Ago and Many Lands.* Boston: Beacon Press, 1948. This book gives forty-two stories that are broadly representative of many lands and cultures.

Jones, Elizabeth B. *When You Need a Special Story.*

Anderson, Ind.: Warner Press, 1959. This book has stories for special occasions and other stories, including seven from the Bible.

Brown, Jeanette Perkins. *The Storyteller in Religious Education.* United Church Press, 1951. This book deals chiefly with the art of telling stories to children and young people, but also has a collection of stories as a forty-two-page appendix.

Kelsey, Alice Geer. *Stories for Junior Worship* (1941) and *Stories of Yesterday and Today for Juniors* (1961). Nashville: Abingdon Press.

Missionary stories for telling and for reading by the pupils may be found in the publications of the Department of Education for Mission, National Council of Churches (Friendship Press). These and other aids for missionary education are made available through the denominational distribution agencies.

YOUTH: In addition to stories which may be found in the resources already listed, leaders are referred in particular to the excellent books of stories that have been written or compiled by Alice A. Bays, of which the following are examples: *Worship Services for Junior Highs, Worship Programs and Stories for Young People, Worship Programs in the Fine Arts.* These are all published by Abingdon Press.

SERMONS FOR CHILDREN

Preaching to children, or to a mixed congregation including children, is an art in which few ministers are proficient—by their own admission. Nevertheless it is an art which they must practice if they are to conduct family services or have a children's message in the general service.

A children's sermon is subject to the rule of all preaching—it should express the minister's own thought and conviction. Since the story-sermon is an appropriate form, the suggestions which have already been made to worship leaders will be useful also to ministers. Some ministers seek help from what others have done in preaching to children —examples, stimulation, and basic ideas. There are many books of children's sermons. Unfortunately most of them are unique to the personality and style of the person who created them and therefore not very useful to anyone else. The following are suggested as useful resources—not so much as a source for children's sermons but as a guide to the minister's own dealing with this difficult problem.

Mielke, Arthur W. *Sermons on Questions Children Ask* (rev. ed.). New York: Thomas Y. Crowell Co., 1963. The book is unique in that the author has paired each children's sermon with one for adults, which expands the same theme and was preached in the same service.

Rest, Karl H. A. *Our Good Enemies.* Philadelphia: United Church Press, 1964. This book contains twenty-five story-sermons by a pastor who is skillfully adept in ministry to children, and whose messages to them have relevance also to those who are older.

Coffin, Henry Sloane. *The Public Worship of God* (out of print). Philadelphia: Westminster Press, 1946. Chapter 9 on "Children and Public Worship" has many fruitful suggestions for talks to children.

INDEX